The Eyes

of

Hierarchy

How the Masters Watch and Help Us

Torkom Saraydarian

N E W   V I S I O N

NVP

P U B L I S H I N G

252 Roadrunner Drive
Sedona, Arizona 86336

Cover Design: Geralyn Cronin
Cover Photo: Mike Basmajian
Printed by: Gilliland Printing

Publisher's Cataloguing-in-Publication
Saraydarian, Torkom.
The eyes of hierarchy : how the masters watch and help us /
Torkom Saraydarian. -- 1st ed.
p. cm.
Includes bibliographical references and index.
Library of Congress Catalogue Number: 97-069851
ISBN: 0-9656203-3-6

1. Ascended masters.   2. Spiritual life.   I. Title.

BP565.S27E94 1998   299.9
                                                       QBI97-30392

Printed in the United States of America

TABLE OF CONTENTS

Merging into the waves of the Infinite, we may be compared to flowers torn away by a storm. How shall we find ourselves transfigured in the ocean of the Infinite?

It would be unwise to send out a boat without a rudder. But the Pilot is predestined and the creation of the heart will not be precipitated into the abyss. Like milestones on a luminous path, the Brothers of Humanity, ever alert, are standing on guard, ready to lead the traveler into the chain of ascent.

Hierarchy is not coercion, it is the law of the Universe. It is not a threat, but the call of the heart and a fiery admonition directing toward the General Good.

Thus, let us cognize the Hierarchy of Light.

Hierarchy, preface
Agni Yoga Society

PREFACE

For me, Masters are not supernatural beings, but beings like other men on the street who worked very hard and eventually, life after life, became influential people in Their field. They became leaders of nations. They became encyclopedic minds, geniuses, and more. This is the human life. You go forward and become a tower instead of a ruin.

In all departments of labor we have prominent men, leaders, and geniuses who love humanity and work for humanity. These are Masters or candidates for mastership. Their method is to work, make efforts, aspire, steadily improve, forge ahead, step on their old self, and strive for new horizons. We have such people. Such people are Masters. They are the embodiment of beauty.

The average man, out of his jealousy, the influence of the media, out of his suspicions, does not recognize such people. It is a sin for him to see beyond his arm. But They exist everywhere, in every nation. Often the characters mentioned in newspapers are failures. The "superman" is not out there somewhere, but he exists next to us in restaurants, on trains, everywhere.

Masters are not a figment of the imagination. It is not a mistake to look at a beautiful girl or boy and say, "My goodness, I see in her or him a future Master, a full-bloomed flower."

This is not wrong, because that girl or that boy will advance in spite of events and, life after life, will reach perfection — mastery. This is the law of Nature. Everything must reach perfection. This is the joy of life.

Many books are written about the Masters. The information in this book is taken from books by the Agni Yoga Society, from the Alice A. Bailey books, from the works of H.P. Blavatsky, and the books by Master Hilarion.

If you want more detailed information about the Masters read

— *The Externalisation of the Hierarchy* by Alice A. Bailey

— *Hierarchy* and *Supermundane* published by the Agni Yoga Society

— *The Secret Doctrine* and *Isis Unveiled* by H.P. Blavatsky

— *The Teachings of the Temple* by Master Hilarion

These books will give you detailed information about the Masters, Who are the Instructors and Protectors of humanity. They stand for us as visions on the path of Light.

In studying this literature you will have first-hand information about the Masters, and then be in a position to reject information which does not correspond to your reason, logic, and intuition.

Torkom Saraydarian

1

THE HIERARCHY[1]

Hierarchy is composed of those human beings who succeeded in mastering their physical, emotional, and mental natures and in expanding their consciousness. The members of the Hierarchy are found on various levels, and They have various tasks and responsibilities.

The guiding star that leads a person into the Hierarchy is the response that he feels in his heart to the Will of God, to the Purpose of God. It is true that one cannot define and explain the Divine Will until he is a Master, but that Will, like a magnet, touches the ready hearts and attracts them upon the path of perfection.

As a person responds more clearly and wholeheartedly to the Will of God, he imposes changes in his life and causes transformation in his nature. Eventually his contact with the Divine Will increases to such a degree that he enters into a process of total transfiguration.

---

1. First published in *Challenge for Discipleship,* Ch. 57.

Sometimes the Divine Will is the Call that a person hears or senses. This Call gradually takes the person, step by step, to the portal of the Hierarchy.

We are told that the members of the Hierarchy have a supreme task: to penetrate deeper into the Will and Purpose of God and to formulate a Plan for humanity to follow. All religions and instructions given by all saviors and all spiritual leaders of the world are nothing else but efforts to translate the Divine Will into a Plan, which can be used to lead nations and humanity into a higher sphere of consciousness in which they understand more clearly the Will of God and live accordingly.

The Plan of the Hierarchy is formulated in such a way that it

- brings health and happiness to humanity
- inspires humanity toward perfection
- inspires humanity to write and create
- synthesizes all nations
- enables individuals, groups, and eventually all humanity to live on a higher dimension, in conscious contact with Higher Worlds

These are the five cornerstones of the Plan. If humanity understands and lives accordingly, it will not be necessary to have any kind of war, pollution, crime and terrorism, pain and suffering, sickness or death.

Hierarchy is the body of a Soul, and each member of the Hierarchy is rooted in His essence in that Soul. Any Master Who comes from the Hierarchy is from the same Soul. Masters are differentiated in Their forms and Their messages to meet the need of the time, but the essence of Their Teaching is the same — it is pure Light, to lead humanity to the Father's Home, to Shamballa.

In essence, through all the Messengers, it is the Father Who speaks. Those who have ears hear only the Father's voice and filter out the fabrications of ages.

Only through love for the Hierarchy can we build a bridge of communication with the Great Ones. The fire in the heart of the Hierarchy is a point of direct contact with the heart of the Universe. This fire is the furnace through which man enters his own Divine heritage.

How can we increase our love for the Hierarchy and thus build the bridge of communication? We increase our love

- by developing a love of Beauty, Goodness, Righteousness, Joy, and Freedom
- by contemplating upon the One Life in all living forms and exercising respect, gratitude, and love for the One Life in every living form
- by understanding the labor of the Hierarchy
- by seeing in each member of the Hierarchy the vision of our future development
- by realizing the help given by Them throughout millions of years in every department of human endeavor
- by realizing that the Hierarchy is the link between humanity and its future achievements on the Cosmic path
- by realizing the extent of the sacrifice of each member of the Hierarchy
- by realizing that the Hierarchy stands for the whole of humanity and for each member of humanity, without discrimination
- by realizing to what extent the Hierarchy shields humanity from attacks of chaotic forces and from its own insanity, to allow it to develop its Divine potentials
- by realizing how the Hierarchy welcomes anyone who has a loving heart

Love is not a sentiment or emotion but the spirit of active sacrificial service to unite humanity, to heal, to free, to transform, and to create. Love toward the members of the Hierarchy expresses itself as a dedicated service to the Plan of the Hierarchy.

Only by developing love toward the Hierarchy can we create the bridge of communication with Them. It is through such a bridge that beauty, joy, and freedom will reach us and the wisdom of the Hierarchy will guide us.

Daily we must take time to raise our hearts to the Hierarchy and increase our love toward the Great Ones. Any action taken against love on any level with any living form weakens the bridge and hinders the communication.

Sometimes we think that we can love the Hierarchy without expressing real love toward our family members, friends, and other human beings. This is called hypocrisy by Christ. No one can love the Hierarchy without loving all that exists. Family quarrels, hatred, and jealousy create cleavages to a great extent between you and the Hierarchy. The first cleavage occurs between you and your Guardian, then between you and the Hierarchy, and then cleavages spread throughout your chain of relationships.

In advanced Teachings, we are told that any cleavage in our life creates rents in our aura and in the communication network between us and the Universe. Love is the substance through which all bridges between the individualized lives and their Source are built. This is why we are told that love unifies.

Reason and logic cannot unify people. Any problem between people must first be approached with love. It is in the light of love that reason and logic can function along their proper lines. Many problems remain unsolved not because of lack of knowledge, reason, and logic, but because of lack of love.

12

There are thousands of examples in our lives in which one moment of love solves our problems when a hundred nights filled with worry and anxiety could not help. Thus, love builds bridges and expands our consciousness and beingness. Actually, it expands our existence in various dimensions.

Communication with Higher Worlds will be established only through love. The Hierarchy can only be reached through a fiery love of the beauty which the Hierarchy expresses.

Love is the flow of the essence between two centers which are magnetically related to each other. Love starts with a dot and turns into a line. This line rotates and revolves around the point and creates a sphere. Love expands as a sphere and eventually makes the human heart the Heart of Cosmos.

People expect the Hierarchy to impose Its will upon humanity. Such an imposition will create many failures on many levels. Imposition is not necessary when the bridge of love is established. Through this bridge, one sees the image of the future achievements. One sees the hindrances in his life and feels the urge to follow the Plan of the Hierarchy. As love increases, the will to serve and be a part of the Plan increases.

Communication with the Hierarchy gradually makes one silent about personal claims. Deeper contact with the Hierarchy makes a person a greater source of love, patience, solemnity, and nobility. In deeper contact with the Hierarchy, the ego and self-interest dissolve. Before these signs appear in the daily life of a person, he cannot be allowed to come in direct and conscious contact with the members of the Hierarchy.

We are told that the Hierarchy is always ready to advise and extend Their hands to humanity. We are told that Their contact with human beings occurs in five stages:

1. We unconsciously feel Their direction.

2. We have a conscious contact with Them.

3. We consciously participate in labor and communicate with Them.

4. We work directly with Them.

5. We commune with Them acting as a member of the Hierarchy. This fifth stage is participation in the joy, bliss, and vision They receive from still Higher Sources.

All these stages are built by the intensification of love. Love for the Hierarchy leads the person into the heart of the Hierarchy and makes him an outpost of the light of the Hierarchy and an executor of the Law of the Hierarchy.

The Law of the Hierarchy refers to the way the Hierarchy operates. Its members vary according to Their level of beingness, Their accomplished labor, and the degree of Their relationship with Higher Centers.

The Hierarch is the supervisor and the representative of the specific Plan to be worked out in the Hierarchy. All members of the Hierarchy receive Their inspiration and courage from the Hierarch.

The link higher than you on the chain of the Hierarchy is your leader. The higher link is your vision. The lower link is your responsibility and the object of your undivided love.

Hierarchical behavior has its own ceremonies in which the Hierarch heads all movements. He is not only the foundation but also the spearhead of all efforts. It is through Him that energies from Higher Sources are received and distributed in the Hierarchy. Also, it is He Who faces the attacks of dark forces and their pressures.

Each member of the Hierarchy has three main tasks:

1. To inspire or train certain members of humanity to strive toward the sphere of the Hierarchy

2. To serve in the Hierarchy in the department where He fits

3. To strive toward higher levels, or prepare Himself for the path of higher evolution

Thus, each member tries not only to serve but also to learn from His Teacher-Master the lessons for higher achievements.

The principle of the Hierarchy, which is inspired by the Divine Purpose, is incessant labor and sacrifice. The Will of Shamballa is the ruling principle in the Hierarchy. This principle is expressed as the fiery spirit of the Hierarchy.

In the Hierarchy, the Law of Oneness is an actualized way of living and working. Everything is done for the harmony of all.

We are told that the externalization of the Hierarchy has three phases:

1. Preparation of individuals and nations to receive the spirit of Christ and manifest it through right human relations and goodwill

2. The appearance of an increasing number of male and female disciples who demonstrate in their lives and teaching an advanced intellect, a pure intuition, an irresistible, Divine will, and a life of dedication and beauty

3. The appearance of certain members of the Hierarchy to prepare the path for the reappearance of Christ

Disciples in the world at this time have three main labors:

1. To demonstrate the beauty of the spiritual life

2. To educate the public about the laws and principles of the spiritual life, in all fields of human endeavor

3. To prepare the hearts and minds of people for the reappearance of Christ, Who promised, by His own words, to come back to the world of men

As with all matters of life, the subject of the reappearance of Christ became a subject of exploitation, deceit, and claims, and here and there the servants of darkness proclaimed, "He is here; He is there." Or they presented themselves as agents or messengers of Christ. Some even dared to proclaim themselves as the Christ. For all these servants of darkness, Christ spoke 2,000 years ago and said:

Then, if anyone says to you, "Look, here is the Messiah," or "There he is," do not believe it. Impostors will come claiming to be messiahs or prophets, and they will produce great signs and wonders to mislead, even God's chosen, if such a thing were possible. See, I have forewarned you. If they tell you, "He is there in the wilderness," do not go out; or if they say, "He is there in the inner room," do not believe it. Like lightening from the east, flashing as far as the west, will be the coming of the Son of Man. . . .

But about that day and hour no one knows, not even the angels in heaven, not even the Son; only the Father.[2]

The Hierarchy is the august body of the disciples of Christ, who stand as a guardian wall between humanity and the Satanic powers of chaos. It is through Their protection and light that individuals find their way into the Kingdom of Heaven through dedicated and sacrificial service for humanity.

The externalization of the Hierarchy is primarily the externalization of virtues, spiritual qualities, and the power of the Inner Glory. The externalization of the Hierarchy is the externalization, actualization, and widespread adaptation of all those laws and principles which Christ taught.

Actually, the laws and principles which He emphasized are slowly penetrating into the soul of humanity and working through world politicians, educators, philosophers, artists, scientists, religious people, and financiers. Great disciples have been born and are being born in all these fields, to carry on and express those principles which will eventually lead

---

2. Matthew 24:23-27, 36

humanity into unity, peace, prosperity, health, and happiness.

People think that the externalization of the Hierarchy means the expansion of religions and the appearance of religious figures. In reality, the externalization of the Hierarchy is a process going on in every field of human endeavor.

People think of Christ as the founder of a religion. This is such a narrow concept. He was a great physician, scientist, political giant, artist, orator, hero — a man of the highest spiritual attainments. All fields of human progress are close to His heart, and in all fields He has His disciples who carry on the great task of advancing science, education, religion, economics, arts, philosophy, and so on.

Thus, Christ is not the head of a religion. He is not even the head of all religions but the Chief Executive of the planetary workshops, and in each of these workshops He has His representatives.

How are His representatives differentiated? The answer is easy. They are not those who say, "Lord, Lord," or those who use His name daily a thousand times to cover their misery. His representatives are those who in every department express utmost honesty, highest dedication, self-renunciation, and heroism. They are those who pursue greater knowledge, who seek right human relations, goodwill, peace, unity, harmony, and justice among all nations.

They are those who have vision, who think about the children of the future and about the health of the planet, about distant worlds. Their prayers are dedicated labor and honesty. They may know about Him, or they may not even remember Him. It does not make any difference to Him, as long as they are doing the Father's Will, through every step of their labor. Expansion of consciousness, education, and creativity are their daily ceremonies. His representatives are those who worship accuracy and discipline. They do not create fantasy but walk on the path of facts and reality.

There are twelve fundamental signs by which you can recognize the servants of the Hierarchy.

1. *The first sign is nobility*. A servant of the Hierarchy is noble in his thoughts, words, and actions. He is noble in all his relations. Nobility is gained when one lives according to the rules and principles of the Hierarchy, when he lives in the presence of the "Watching Eye."

A noble person is solemn, serene, self-controlled, accurate, wise, and highly educated. When you meet a noble person, you know that he is here on earth to bring Beauty, Goodness, Righteousness, Joy, and Freedom.

2. *The second sign is striving toward perfection*. He demonstrates ongoing labor to perfect his personality, his creativity, his relationships, his knowledge. He tries continuously to advance his state of consciousness. No servant of the Hierarchy is lazy. They are all rhythm. They are like currents; they are rhythmically active.

3. *The third sign is progressiveness in his outlook*. He thinks for the future; he plans for the future without ignoring past and present conditions. It is the future vision that inspires him to plan, to decide, and to organize. He is not stuck in past outlooks. He does not ignore past values, but he always searches for new ways and means to bring greater light and love and better relationships in all departments of human endeavor.

He lives with new-age thinking. He does not repeat old-age habits, behaviors, and attitudes. He always tries to create something new that better fits his vision of the future.

He may be found in any field, and in that field he stands as the call of the future. He exercises a moral pressure in his environment. He does not force people, but his presence makes them work and try to advance toward the future.

4. *The fourth sign is inclusiveness*. He is not separative. We are not referring only to racial discrimination. An inclusive person not only respects the existence of other people but also is open to new ideas, new visions, new knowledge, and new ways of doing things which are more goal-fitting.

He is not crystallized in his beliefs and traditions. He respectfully approaches all traditions and all opinions, as well as the labor, culture, and traditions of other people, and he sees beauty, meaning, future, and usefulness in them. The Hierarchy stands for all, for every path of research, for every genuine experience. For a servant of the Hierarchy, any knowledge in any field is precious.

Hierarchy stands for inclusiveness. Like a mother hen, a servant of the Hierarchy collects the chicks under his wings. Every nation has its beautiful culture. A servant of the Hierarchy respects all cultures. He not only respects them, but also tries to understand, love, and enjoy them. Inclusiveness is the progressive endeavor to bring unity and synthesis.

5. *The fifth sign is creativeness* — creativity in everything: in ideas, in thoughts, in speech, in manners, in art, in business, at home. In all these and other areas, a servant of the Hierarchy manifests creativity.

Creativity means to build those ways and means which can meet the growing needs of humanity, which can meet the rising consciousness of humanity, which can meet the expanding sense of beauty of humanity. Such people are not satisfied with what they are and what they can do. They forge ahead and seek new ideas, new visions, new inspirations, new impressions, and new revelations. They try to actualize these things in new forms, new activities, and new relationships, to meet the rising needs of humanity and to offer a new vision to the expanding consciousness of humanity.

6. *The sixth sign is honesty*. Without honesty, one cannot lead, inspire, create trust, or radiate light. Any action to exploit human beings with any idea, proposal, or attitude creates dire consequences and undermines the cause.

No one can be called a servant of the Hierarchy if he has not graduated with honesty from the School of Life. A servant of the Hierarchy is honest in his thoughts, words, and actions. Honesty is a sign that a person is free from the influences of his lower self and the lower selves of others. Such a person is honest, not because others are crooked or honest but because it is his nature to be honest.

Honesty imposes harmony and rhythm and brings the influence of the Hierarchy in those areas where honest people live.

7. The seventh sign is freedom from prejudice. The mind of a servant of the Hierarchy is not controlled by what people are, do, or say. He has his own light, and in that light he functions. The thoughts, words, actions, and behavior of other people do not obscure his light. He does not give them power to condition him by reacting according to their expectations. He manifests beauty, goodness, justice, joy, and freedom without being conditioned by those who try to impose upon him their standards and moods.

In a deeper sense, to be free from prejudice means to be free to act in the light of Beauty, Goodness, Righteousness, Joy, and inclusiveness. A person who is free from prejudice does not hurt you because you hurt him, but he cares for you more because you hurt him. He tries to find any avenue to enlighten you, to expand your consciousness, and to help you free yourself from your limitations. This is a part of his service.

8. The eighth sign is freedom from vanity and ego. These two vices go together. Every egotist is full of vanity. Actually, ego is formed by images of vanity.

A servant of the Hierarchy is free from vanity. He knows himself exactly as he is. He knows exactly what he has or does not have. He knows exactly what he can do and what he cannot do. Ego sets false measures before your eyes and in your mind. A servant of the Hierarchy is a clear person, and because he does not have vanity and ego, he sees exactly what others are. But instead of judging and condemning others, he tries to enlighten them by his example and beauty.

Vanity and ego serve their owner. A servant of the Hierarchy serves others and tries to save them and uplift them. He tries to bring people to their senses. You cannot defeat a servant of the Hierarchy by your mistakes or failures. You cannot defeat him by your works of darkness. He cannot be defeated because one can be defeated only when he has vanity and ego.

9. *The ninth sign is righteousness*. Righteousness is the substance by which a servant of the Hierarchy is built. People think that righteousness is a virtue learned in earthly life, whereas its true origin lies in the standards impressed in one's soul while in the Subtle Worlds. The assimilation of true values in the Subtle Worlds flourishes as righteousness in the earthly incarnations.

It is not easy to teach someone to be righteous, but when he has the experience of true values, he is naturally righteous. The servants of the Hierarchy are righteous in all their thinking, expressions, and relationships because they know the Law of Karma and they know about the principles dominating in the Subtle Worlds.

The Great Ones do not advertise Themselves. By Their fruits you recognize Them. Hierarchical personnel do not think about Themselves as bodies, forms, or personalities. They think about Themselves as ideas, directions, currents of energy, virtues, or lights. People call Them by many names, and each of Them is called by many other names. But They are not names, pictures, or images. They are principles, sources of beauty and guidance and visions for the future.

In Their real states They are like symphonies, arrows of energy, bridges between worlds, rainbows between shores. Limiting Them in human form and making Them only images of human weakness or making Them so abstract that the human imagination cannot conceive Them is to work against the work They are trying to do which is to build a bridge between what man is now and what he can be in the future.

10. *The tenth sign is faithfulness to the human cause.* A servant of the Hierarchy tries to bring humanity together and protect humanity from serpents and coyotes. He cares for the survival of humanity and its future perfection. He cares for the planet so that the planet is healthy and able to nourish its children.

He suffers with those who suffer at the hands of powerful people. He tries to inspire in them the spirit of freedom and liberation. For him, there is no cause higher than the cause of humanity, and he can subordinate all his interests to the global interest.

Such people are not rare any more. You can find their numbers increasing everywhere.

11. *The eleventh sign is sacrifice and heroism.* In the smallest labor, the servant of the Hierarchy demonstrates a sacrificial spirit, and in the time of crisis the spirit of heroism radiates out from him. He demonstrates courage, fearlessness, and daring. He sacrifices his time, money, properties, and even his life if necessary. He lives a dangerous life, but he is not a fool; he is not careless. He is cautious and extremely observant. He knows that life is dangerous, and he also knows that the shortest and fastest path is the most dangerous path.

12. *The twelfth sign is goodness or goodwill.* A servant of the Hierarchy wishes good for all, even for those who cannot live according to his standards. He thinks good, speaks good, and acts for good, without discrimination, because he knows that in having complete goodwill, he transmits the will of the One Who rules the Universe.

Every true disciple is a servant of the Hierarchy.

The Hierarchy is a source of goodness. All that They try to do is to teach people to be good, to express goodwill, and never to violate this principle with their thoughts, words, or actions.

We are told that those who attained Masterhood are those who, for thousands of years, did not fall into the traps of malice, slander, and treason. The existence of such vices in any human being immediately reveals that he is not a worker of the Hierarchy, no matter in what dress or position he presents himself.

Goodness is the foundation of the life of a Hierarchical worker. When you find such a person, you feel safe, protected, and blessed.

There are also twelve signs by which you can immediately recognize those so-called Hierarchical workers who are actually wolves in sheepskin.

1. *A worker of the Hierarchy does not make claims*. He does not say he is a Master or a great Initiate. He lets people find out exactly what he is. Any claim proves that he has not yet been admitted into the closer ranks of the Hierarchy, or that he is a merchant of vanity and self-interest.

A claim-maker tries to superimpose his own image upon you, to give you the impression that he is a Great One. Such people are very poor in their hearts. "By the fruit of them you will know them."

2. *A Hierarchical worker never speaks about the details of his past lives, nor is he interested in the past lives of others*. Being closer to the Hierarchy, he knows that it is the future that is important, not the past. It is the future that calls the soul upward toward perfection and beauty.

Advanced people do not even like to look back because they do not want to re-stimulate memories from the past before all memories are rendered harmless. Hierarchical workers do not want to be influenced by the past and by those who were with them in different relationships. They want to make new choices, to test their intuition, and to forge ahead toward success and victory.

It is possible that your Teacher, a Great One, or your Solar Angel reveals to you a portion of a past life for a certain, specific reason. But even in this case, you do not have the right to speak to others about your past lives.

We are told that even great Chohans are not allowed to be interested in the past lives of people except when, for Ashramic reasons, They study, by permission, certain of your lives to see if you are really ready to handle severe responsibilities and if you are capable of carrying a heavy voltage of energy.

3. *Hierarchical workers do not speak about their inner relationships with the Great Ones*. They do not use the names of Great Ones to collect money, to build reputations, or to influence people. Such steps are ugly steps. Advanced workers are hard workers, and they do not need to take advantage of their relationship with Higher Forces.

4. *A worker of the Hierarchy never talks about his rank in relation to others*. You hear many people saying things like: "I am the commander of the space-people." "I am the ruler of angels." "I just took the Fifth Initiation." "I made a visit to the Holy Ashram." All such claims create barriers on the path of humanity, and intelligent people feel deep repulsion. Do not forget: By their fruit you will know people.

5. *A worker of the Hierarchy does not reveal anything about your past lives nor does he read your aura to show off or to gain influence or money*. It is possible that a worker of the Hierarchy, on some rare occasions, reveals a part of your past life for specific instruction or to point out a defect in your aura, as a warning. The worker of the Hierarchy is mostly interested in the future expansion of your consciousness, rather than in your past.

The disciples of the world must be very careful not to listen to those charlatans who read people's auras and tell them about their past lives without having the real capacity or a reason to do it. Until one develops higher clairvoyance and passes the Initiation of Transfiguration, his readings are false, inaccurate, misleading, and mixed with millions of impressions floating in space.[3]

6. A Hierarchical worker never imposes his will upon others. He never violates the free will of people. He pays a heavy karma if he does. He also does not give direct advice and expect obedience.

For example, a Hierarchical worker does not tell you to marry a certain person or divorce someone, or to have children or not to have children. He does not use his psychic powers to direct people the way he wants. On the contrary, the Hierarchical worker tries to make people independent and free. He helps them make decisions and solve problems, but He never decides for them or solves their problems for them.

A Hierarchical worker helps people by illuminating their minds, expanding their consciousness, and enabling them to see their problems from various viewpoints. He suggests books, schools, and teachers, and he helps them to stand on their own feet.

No one is allowed to interfere with the karma of another person. This is a very delicate subject. The Hierarchical worker is always ready to help, but he does not force his will upon others or violate their free will or karma.

7. The Hierarchical worker never discriminates between religions. He knows that all religions are given by the Hierarchy to meet various needs of various levels of people at various times. But he honors the religion he was born into without having antagonism toward any other religion. If he meets strangers who do not belong to his religion, he discusses their religion with them and tries to reveal to them the

---

3. See *The Psyche and Psychism*, Ch. 21, and *Breakthrough to Higher Psychism*, Ch. 1, to read about higher clairvoyance; see *Cosmos in Man*, Ch. 19, to read about past lives.

deeper layers of their religion, thus enriching and expanding their consciousness.

The Hierarchical worker knows that all religions are given to all nations as paths toward perfection. No Hierarchical worker imposes his beliefs upon others. For him, the important thing is to see how people live and not what they believe.

Those who work within the walls of dogmas, doctrines, and crystallized traditions will be limited within the walls built by the achievements of those who created them. Our thinking must be free to achieve new heights. Our horizon must be limitless, to allow us to expand our consciousness. In forcing on others the limits of our thinking and beliefs, or our accepted doctrines, dogmas, and traditions, we not only limit people and create barriers on the path of their progress but also paralyze our own progress.

8. *A Hierarchical worker never exploits people or misuses them*. For him, every person is sacred. He does not lie to people or bribe them to gain votes. He is righteous in his relationships, and he does not want to burden his karma by using others for his personal gains.

Your children can be servants of the Hierarchy. If you raise them in the right way, you will see how much beauty they will introduce into life.

9. *A Hierarchical worker never displays psychic phenomena*, and if he does use his psychic powers in secret to save a person, he gives the credit to God. The Hierarchical worker never uses his psychic powers to influence people, to create attraction or recognition, or to impose his image on others. The powers he has are sacred, and he uses them only for the benefit of others if their karma permits.

If in rare cases he uses his powers, he does it to glorify the Source of all powers. His existence among people is a blessing. His aura, his look, and his touch heal people and enlighten and strengthen them. It is known that the presence of a Hierarchical worker can prevent earthquakes and natural catastrophes. Hierarchical workers are often sent to certain places to protect people from natural upheavals by their presence. They are sent to restore peace and understanding, to bring health and prosperity, but they remain unknown until people develop eyes to see their influence.

10. The Hierarchical worker is economical. He never wastes his or others' energy, money, time, and so on, because he knows that waste builds karma and creates attachment. When one wastes money, energy, time, and matter, it means that he has not yet learned the value of what he has. And if he does not know the value of what he has, he wastes it or locks it up. In both cases, he works against the law. The Law of Economy means to use all that exists properly, for the purpose of perfection.

Wasting is a taxation on Nature, and it puts a burden on others. Nature is misused and overexploited because of waste. When Nature is exploited by wasting, we have smog; we have poison; we have radioactivity. Economy is balance between Nature and human need.

11. A Hierarchical worker never associates himself with mediums and channels. He knows that the source of their inspiration is not higher spheres but doubtful entities and astral forces. He knows that a contact with them may be fatal because they often create a permanent line through which they keep him captive to the demands of destructive forces.[4]

12. The Hierarchical worker never tries necromancy. He leaves the dead free to proceed on their way toward the Higher Worlds. Instead of asking for help and direction from them, he tries to lead them toward light through his elevated thoughts. A worker of the Hierarchy knows how to contact them mentally and help their evolution. He can even be with them after he leaves his body while sleeping. But he never

---

4. See *Cosmos in Man*, Ch. 21.

tries to bring them to the earth and make them reverse their direction.

People may ask, "If the workers of the Hierarchy are so beautiful, why don't we see more changes in life in general?" The answer is simple. First, there are enormous changes occurring, changes toward unity, beauty, synthesis, and peace. Second, it is because of the increasing presence of Hierarchical workers that so many conflicts are coming to the surface. Goodwill makes people see the existing ill will. Freedom makes people see where the freedom of humanity is being violated. Unity reveals cleavages and existing separatism. Light reveals the darkness.

This is why the world is entering the "midnight hour." It is only in the midnight hour that the dawn will start, and this will be the victory of all Forces of Light and of all those who work in the light and for light.

Every disciple is a herald of light, a light that shines in darkness — through his self-sacrifice, through the warmth of his heart, through the penetrating light of his consciousness, and through the power and beauty of the flame of his soul. His mission is to shine the light. His flame will be steady and strong, even if the wind, the rain, and the snow rage around him during dark nights and stormy days. It is during these days that he will prove his power of fusion with the Divine Flame, which will continuously provide the strength to persist against the chaotic elements of Nature.

Only those who keep their flame lit during stormy days will be able to build the mechanism through which it will be possible to make a breakthrough into the Higher Worlds. A disciple is a progressing light in the darkness of night and in the darkness of day.

2

HOW THE MASTERS SERVE

They research and investigate, analyze, and synthesize. They are the students of Kosmos. They are perfect from the viewpoint of human beings.

They are beginners from the viewpoint of the Cosmic Astral Plane. Human evolution is carried on upon the Cosmic Physical Plane. There are six other Cosmic Planes to be traveled on. Masters are active in the Cosmic Physical Plane.

They have committed Themselves to serve humanity, and twenty-four hours a day They try to meet the needs of humanity.

They live on earth with Their physical or etheric bodies but They have higher bodies for higher planes. They can be sick and cured with Their own methods.

They never interfere in human actions, except if, behind an action, Satan works.

They are warriors in the sense that They fight against chaotic elements in all strata. They fight against ignorance, superstition, prejudice, and darkness. They fight by the sword of Light — in courage and fearlessness.

They closely follow planetary events. They live on this planet in remote places. One or two of Them help great nations or groups of nations. They travel all over the world. They are in instant communication with each other.

They inspire those who serve humanity. They inspire those artists who bring beauty in any form. They help scientists if they are spiritually oriented. They look for leaders and inspire them to right direction.

They never interfere with the karma of people. They want people to solve their own problems and choose their own path with their own free will. But They send the light of wisdom, knowing that some will accept and some will reject.

They protect Their agents of light in the world. They, as a group, build a shield between chaotic forces of Nature and the human race. They are called Shepherds.

They help Their disciples to expand their consciousness and penetrate into the mysteries of life. They closely observe the physical, emotional, mental, and spiritual activities of Their disciples. They are sensitive even to the flash of a thought.

With special ceremonies, They admit or initiate disciples to higher levels of consciousness and reveal greater mysteries to them.

They heal people, if healing will not violate the karma of the person. They heal mostly by sending their special energies or frequencies or by leading people to places or persons in order to find the means to heal themselves.

They meditate on solar, galactic, and Kosmic mysteries. They are travelers on the path of Infinity. They not only work on the physical plane, but serve also in the astral and mental planes, where those who have left their bodies exist.

Some of the Masters are great painters, sculptors, organizers of rhythmic dances and movements. Some of Them are inventors. Some inventors on earth are impressed by Them. They have apparatuses to amplify thought currents or register the thoughts of others. They have apparatuses that work by psychic energy.

Some of Them are mathematicians. Some are linguists. There are also those Who are supreme financiers. It is These people who move humanity forward through Their thought currents when they are accepted.

We are told that the leader of the Hierarchy is Christ. All His coworkers are His disciples. The Hierarchy was formed by a Great Being Who is named the Ancient of Days. As a collective body They offer a plan to humanity — a constitution which if understood and followed will help humanity to have health, happiness, success, peace, and freedom on earth and pass to the fifth kingdom and enjoy the glory awaiting them in the future. All Masters do not work in the Hierarchy. After They are trained in it, They pass on to different labors in the Universe.

Masters are not omnipresent, omniscient, and omnipotent individuals. They are relatively imperfect, striving toward perfection. But They belong to the fifth kingdom. The difference between general humanity and Masters is the difference between the human and animal kingdoms. They call Themselves the Elder Brothers of humanity.

Masters are fully clairvoyant and clairaudient. This means They can see the astral and mental planes as clearly as They can see the physical world. Also, They can hear conversations or calls or messages coming from the Subtle Worlds. In addition, They can watch the life of Their disciples, their emotional and mental activities if needed.

All this is done to serve people and to guide them.

They are a group and this group is called Hierarchy. They have classes and these classes are called Ashrams. The Hierarchy and the Ashrams exist in the Intuitional Plane. There are many disembodied souls and advanced human beings who can attend these classes. These classes teach all that you can imagine at very advanced levels. Most of the knowledge brought to earth by advanced people are fragments of knowledge given in these classes.

One major subject is wisdom, which is taught in every Ashram. Those who visit Ashrams from earth come back and shine with their beauty, wisdom, and leadership as much as their karma tolerates.

Ashrams receive many souls from space, even from certain planets and systems. All prominent people in the world are students of Their Ashrams. Some of Their students are conscious of the Ashrams; some are not, for their own protection.

Masters have the ability to leave Their physical or etheric body. In Their higher bodies They travel from one planet to another. Many Masters visit other planets daily where people live with their etheric, astral, or mental bodies, and in different forms.

They often visit Their disciples on earth with Their own image and discuss with them urgent matters.

They communicate with Their disciples by telepathically talking with them, or etherically faxing Their important symbols or diagrams. They use the method of impression with Their advanced disciples.

Masters have the ability to take Their disciples to visit various spiritual vortexes on earth and even to different planets to help them expand. They take them in their subtle bodies. Some of the disciples can remember their experiences; some of them cannot. They sense irritation and fear, which burdens Them. They sense our connection to Them and our joy, which gives Them spiritual pleasures.

They look for motives and the quality of service in order to promote Their disciples.

They do not use miracles — They think miracles do not exist. All that happens is the result of cause and effect.

People think that Masters are magicians and miracle

workers, but They work with the Laws of Nature, and They respect these laws. They think scientifically, and all Their operations are based on scientific, clear thinking because Their mind functions beyond the mist and fog of illusions and glamors, prejudices and superstitions.

They do not encourage mediums, channels, or psychics. They think some of these people are sick or are possessed by inferior entities or by the enemies of mankind.

They do not belong to any religion or philosophy. They are all-inclusive.

Their main characteristic is compassion.

They have disciples in all religions and political movements who lead humanity to unity, peace, and freedom.

Masters never give orders or impose Their will upon Their disciples but illuminate them with Their Light.

Masters know that everyone is destined to become a Master in the future, perhaps in thousands of years or in millions of years. Masters hold an image of perfection, a vision for those who are awakened.

Each Master represents a current of Cosmic energy. Each Master has His or Her color, fragrance, and symbol.

There are Masters who have masculine form and Masters Who have feminine form. Masters who have feminine form are called Taras.

In the Hierarchy there are representatives of every race and nation. They show interest in those people on earth who sincerely dedicate themselves to the service of humanity as a whole and who equip themselves with knowledge, purity, and wisdom to accomplish their missions. To be admitted into Their classes one must shine with the light of service for humanity.

Masters do not have real names. They are called by different names in different places and in different ages.

Anyone of us can be a Master by mastering our nature

and striving toward the future.

There are five steps to reach mastery.

▲ purity of heart
▲ meditation
▲ striving toward the highest
▲ compassion
▲ sacrificial service

There are nine signs by which you can know those who are on the path of mastery. They are those who demonstrate

▲ harmlessness
▲ right speech
▲ goodwill
▲ forgiveness
▲ righteousness
▲ joy
▲ freedom
▲ sense of responsibility
▲ commitment

The greatest joy of the Master is to see the formation of masterhood within any man and within any woman.

MASTERS AND THEIR BODIES

We are told that most of the Masters function in Their etheric bodies. But these etheric bodies are made of higher ethers — Buddhic, Atmic, Monadic, and Divine. These are very fine ethers, and they serve as communication apparatuses with Higher Worlds and Other Worlds.

Some of Them still have physical bodies, but Their bodies are rhythmic and made of atomic substance. Those who have physical bodies can leave them at any time when They need to work in higher planes.

Those who have higher etheric bodies shine like rainbows with dazzling light. To come in contact with such bodies is very dangerous, unless you are ready, because Their frequency may burn your centers. They usually communicate with Their disciples by telepathy or by the science of impression or sometimes by direct contact.

Some Masters have families and live a very normal life.

There are also many astral entities, puffed by their ego, vanity, and glamors, who act as masters in the astral plane and cause contact with mediums through their astral nature. Some mediums are fascinated with such entities, and they receive messages of very mediocre or commonplace order, but the zeal of mediums makes these entities "famous" and important. When the time comes for the entities to move on to the mental plane, their communication stops. Only the astral corpses communicate with the mediums for a while in a progressively degenerating manner.

A real Master follows a plan with His disciples, mostly guiding them to fields of greater service and sacrifice. Their influence and power grow through Their instruction and guidance and continue life after life.

MASTERS WHO SUFFER

One may ask, do Masters suffer? They do. In Their long, dangerous life, They are exposed to many dangers — physical danger, psychic danger, and mental danger. Their equipment is so sensitive that They register the slightest animosity, dark emotions, and thoughts. They pass through conditions in which are found many traps of the dark forces and their agents. By all means the darkness tries to eliminate the servants of Light. Only Their vigilance and good deeds protect Them.

Those who enjoy Their company often betray Them and serve darkness. Others try to waste Their time or misdirect Them so that They do not fulfill Their destiny.

We are told that many times They change Their locations so as not to be recognized. Walking toward unlimited perfection, They try to discipline Themselves in everything because They know that without discipline darkness is not conquered. Survival of the fittest is a great law. They try to fit Themselves to advancing life and the expanding horizons of a new consciousness.

People visualize Masters as sitting in paradise and enjoying the bountifulness of life. It is true that in one part of Their consciousness They are in incessant joy, but the other part of Their consciousness is in the world of sorrow and pain and suffering.

Sometimes They notice how a disciple is suffering within his karma, and They can only extend Their hand of joy, being unable to do anything more for him.

Their suffering is so deep, especially at the time of war. No one can see the suffering of babies, widows, and families as clearly as They see it. They hasten to help them, but the need is beyond Their capacity sometimes. Their golden heart bleeds, and Their tears appear as red blood. They do not play the harp with angels. They really re-experience human suffering.

3

HOW TO CONTACT YOUR MASTER

We can come in contact with a Master through the following steps:

The first step is to purify your physical body, emotional body, and mental body. This means you will abstain from crimes, wrong actions, harmful actions, and develop your body to be as healthy as possible. Then you must purify your emotional body from every kind of fear, anger, hatred, jealousy, revenge, and slander. These kinds of emotions pollute your emotional body. Then you must purify your mental body from ego, vanity, fanaticism, separatism, and greed. If these conditions are met, you are in the spotlight of the discipline of the Master.

The second step is meditation.[1]

The third step is full moon observations and five-day preparation for the full moon.[2]

The fourth step is to have a service plan and render service in your field for humanity.

1. See *The Science of Meditation.*
2. See *Symphony of the Zodiac.*

The fifth step is to live a noble and honest life.

The sixth step is to assimilate the Ageless Wisdom as much as possible and live your life accordingly.

The seventh step is to have reverent love for all creation.

If these seven steps are taken, it is impossible for the Master not to meet you in person.

The Masters are like those Who watch on the mountain top at night and look at the valley for any light approaching Them. When They see the light, They hasten to help you climb the mountain to meet your Master.

Masters are anxious to find coworkers. Whoever shows striving and nobility, They do not miss.

Masters are not occupied with your personality interests. They are anxious to find people who will dedicate their lives for the service of humanity, for the betterment of life, for the success of all people. Masters are interested in people who build communication lines with their abstract mind, so that They are able to relate to them.

Masters are not ghosts. They are intelligent executors Who care for coworkers in every field of human labor.

Most Masters are in contact with us, but we are not conscious of it. They guide us through dreams, visions, feelings, and telepathy, but we are ignorant of these efforts.

Above all, the quickest way to meet Them is through devoted, sacrificial service for humanity. This is the shortest way that eventually will take you to Their presence. Magic, mediumism, psychism, hypnotism, channeling, do not lead you to Them but to astral spooks who masquerade as Masters.

If in a previous life, you consciously or unconsciously served humanity and rendered sacrificial service, you are closer to Them than you think. They see that from your innate consciousness and strength you paved your way toward Them for only one reason: to learn how to better serve and cooperate with Their efforts for the transformation of humanity.

Sometimes They contact you every thirty years, once or twice in your short life, but that contact stays with you as a source of strength, inspiration, and courage.

HOW MASTERS SEND MESSAGES

Sometimes, it is like talking to you. You hear a word or a short sentence, but that word or short sentence opens a new horizon in you. The word can become a key for a treasure-house because, besides the word, the word is charged by thoughts pregnant with many treasures. Often these words cannot reach you in their purity and totality. There are many reasons for this. Electromagnetic currents distort them. Some astral and low mental entities swallow them or partially obscure them. It is even possible that some entities mix other messages with them in order to make them confusing and without meaning.

There are some mediums who listen to messages between a Master and disciple, but because of the mediums' unreadiness to grasp the messages, they present to the public something ridiculous or meaningless.

The disciple must prepare to be able to receive telepathic messages from the Master through meditation and silence. If there is no preparation, the reception can be very poor and misleading.

Masters know what time to send a message so as not to be trapped by dark forces or evil entities. It is imperative that a disciple must not drink or dope himself or eat meat because these elements gather around him very nosy and disturbing entities.

It is also possible that messages can be mixed and strange sentences are formed. If the receiver is not attentive, focused, and ready in his heart, communication will not help him.

The science of impression is a higher science than telepathy. It uses a different frequency to be translated in the mind of the receiver the way They want. The equipment of the receiver is specifically organized and ready for it.

Sometimes They communicate with symbols. You see symbols on the wall in various shapes and colors. The symbol stays for one to three minutes, sometimes longer if you are anxious to copy it. These symbols are also subject to the possibility of distortion by atmospheric storms and dark forces, but often the visualization of the Master can overcome all possible obstacles.

Sometimes They communicate through advanced disciples to warn you or to guide you. Many times an advanced disciple is forbidden to give a message from the Master to you. He gives you the message as his message and leaves it with you to accept or reject.

Those who pretend that they are receiving messages and giving messages eventually fall into an often incurable brain sickness. It is a serious responsibility to receive a genuine message and deliver it as if it were your advice.

4

MASTERS AND COWORKERS

There is a certain opinion that Masters work with people whom They knew in the past. This is not completely true. If in the past life someone achieved cooperation with Them and carried out Their burden in a superior way, of course, in coming incarnations They will choose to work with such people because of less expenditure of energy and friction, but not simply because They knew him or them.

If in past lives they harmonized their centers to the will of Great Ones and to the Plan of the Hierarchy, Masters choose such people because it is safer to work with them and achieve greater results. The closer contact blows the fuses of unprepared ones and damages them.

Also, those who were able to coordinate their centers with Great Ones through striving and hard labor, Masters choose these people because of the harmony existing between them.

Masters never favor people. The only key you need is your attainment. Wherever They see readiness, They approach you and invite you for closer labor.

Sometimes a person unknowingly works many incarnations under Their watchful eyes until They decide it is safe to have direct contact with him. This is reaffirmed by true Masters.

Some people in every incarnation do a great sacrifice or labor for Them, to actualize some part of the Plan. They choose such people for Their coworkers. This is human and natural. A person tries to work with those who are cooperative, both psychically and physically, and who suffered many wounds in life and paid a heavy karma for the sake of the Hierarchy.

MASTERS AND DISCIPLES

It was asked why Masters are very careful in choosing disciples. When a person is enlightened to a certain degree and starts to think in terms of one humanity, Masters follow him through Their eyes and suggest that he enter into discipline. The person passes from one discipline to another according to his capacity to endure and create integration in his nature, right human relations with others, and alignment with his Inner Lord.

His training deepens. He learns the science of advanced meditation, visualization, and creative imagination. This takes long years of serious work. Then he learns to build the golden bridge and be sensitive to the thoughts of his Solar Angel and his Master.

Then he learns how to record higher impressions and translate them for the Common Good.

Until the Third Initiation is achieved, the Masters work behind the scenes and indirectly. At the Third Initiation, They call upon him for greater preparation and to greater service. In the Third Initiation, the person starts to think and undergoes a lengthy training about the science of thinking because after the Third Initiation he will mostly work through and with his thoughts.

After the Third Initiation, he will learn the science of battle with dark forces in subtle levels on the physical plane. The dark forces immediately mobilize themselves when someone enters into the Third Initiation. Masters spend a great amount of time and energy protecting the Initiate and teaching the technique of fighting.

From the eyes of the Masters, nothing escapes. They see those who begin to carry Their light and immediately take them under Their protection. The person cannot feel the protection at first, but then slowly he becomes aware that he is being protected from many dangers.

Masters meet him when the time is ripe and when the person is ready to cooperate with all his strength.

The meetings with the Master increase for the disciple as he travels toward the Fourth Initiation, and They establish a deep friendship for the service of humanity.

Masters prepare people directly or indirectly, but always behind the scenes, until they are ready to meet face to face.

The care of the Masters for Their disciples is very deep. They, with whole heart, await their progress and victories so that they become members of the Army of Light.

All sorts of training in life and discipline is necessary if a disciple is going to meet his Hierarchical Master. With this discipline and training, the disciple carries the image of his Master in the center of his heart with deep devotion and dedication through many incarnations. This is very necessary because devotion and dedication prepare him to respond to His radiation slowly until he gets used to it. We are told that the radiation of the Masters is as powerful as the radiation of radium.

The Masters prepare their disciples slowly until they are capable of responding to the radiation in creative ways.

However, disciples feel this invisible presence and try to harmonize with His will and vision.

When the times comes, a Master meets His disciple, and the meeting does not shock him because of the long years of preparation and discipline.

Why are Masters so careful in choosing relations with disciples? A disciple's aura can influence the aura of the Master, and if it is not clean, the Master's aura can damage the aura of the disciple. The disciple's glamors, illusions, and maya must be cleared to some degree in order not to hinder the labor of the Master. The disciple can be overstimulated and become a danger in the environment.

Before the disciple is ready to be with the Master, he must work out his karma.

The Master waits until the disciple is ready and there is no danger in working with him. This requires labor and striving on the part of the disciple.

MASTERS AND SILENCE

Masters have many ways to test a disciple, but the hardest way for a disciple is when They teach him with Their silence, as if the disciple does not exist. They remain secluded in silence toward Their disciple. They not only do not communicate with words but also cut themselves from the aspirant or disciple telepathically. This puts a tremendous tension upon the disciple in which he grows in wisdom and action, if he is a true disciple.

Silence of the Teacher also creates a crisis in which disciples are tested in their devotion, trust, faith, and responsibility toward the Teacher and toward the people around them. Many so-called disciples are dropped from the path, and many of them turn antagonistic toward the Teaching and their Master.

No matter what kind of condition the disciple is passing, the Teacher watches him in silence to see if his inner flame is lit and striving. In a silent period by the Master, the disciple must continue his work enthusiastically without any complaints, but, in the meantime, must be careful not to break in any way the "silver cord" between the Teacher and himself.

There are periods in which the disciple can closely examine his thoughts, emotions, and activities and throw away any unworthy element found within himself. Also, the disciple learns not to lean on his Teacher but has courage and daring to go ahead. He can exercise his ability to stand alone, to make his own decisions, draw his own plans, and act independently from his Teacher but in harmony with the laws and principles.

There are people in the world who, without striving and building merits, expect the Master to baby-sit them, lead them, protect them, teach them. If the Master sees that a person is developing an inclination to hang on Him, He abandons him, until life experience teaches him to be strong and to depend on himself and his own karma.

Some people praise their Master in other ways by giving new shoes, a new home, a good dinner, nice company. This is a naive attitude and does not make the disciple an intelligent worker.

Masters can cut Their relationship with Their disciples if They see that they are disobeying the Law of Love, or if They are living on different globes or are engaged in some emergency. They cut Their relationship to test the attitude of the disciple, or They cut Their relationship to strengthen Their disciple. They have many reasons to do this and an accepted disciple will know Their motives.

Intelligent disciples never waste the energy of their Masters. They do not expect Them to appear to them, give verbal messages, and so on. They know that a tremendous expenditure of energy is utilized by such acts, and they do not become dependent children to Them. On the contrary, they make themselves ready to take some burdens from Their shoulders, thus showing their understanding and love.

People think that Masters choose as Their disciples and

coworkers those who are
- learned in esoteric literature
- devoted to their studies and meditation
- isolated from their groups and friends as if they were outstanding personalities and individuals
- working in churches and in organizations with higher positions
- accumulating lots of people around themselves and making their organization powerful

It is true that a disciple can have deep wisdom and knowledge; he can have a high position and a magnetic aura; he can have vast knowledge about esotericism, but these are not the only criteria by which you are recognized by your Master. In addition, you must have the subjective qualities such as self-abnegation, which is total dedication to the service of humanity and a lack of interest in appreciation and recognition. Masters are interested in people who are self-forgetful in the service of others and honestly striving to become more so that they can meet the needs of the people.

They are humble, noble, law-abiding people. They do not have ego, pride, and vanity. They do not think about their advantage and spiritual progress but seek to serve. They look for people who have control over their speech, and no flattery, praise, or pleasure can loosen their mouths.

They have control over their thoughts, emotions, and activities, so that they are in harmony with the plan "of love and light."

They have strict control over their speech. They know what to say and what not to say. They are noble people. Nobility is a sign that they are subjectively in contact with the Hierarchy.

They are convinced of the Supermundane World, the subjective work, and daily they walk in the light of that world.

The Hierarchy does not choose people for great service

from those who learn, who graduate, who reach positions and power only to save themselves under the pretense of serving others.

Candidates for Hierarchical service believe in the Law of Cause and Effect and live totally under that law because the Hierarchical service cannot be performed until you are actualizing that law to the highest limit.

They do not chose their disciples from those who boast about their knowledge, position, and influence but choose those whose hearts are humble and who exercise self-abnegation and self-renunciation.

Many disciples complain that they do not have any contact with the Hierarchy and wonder why. Even the anxiety of having a contact with Them is an imposition on Them. You live your life through self-forgetfulness, harmlessness, and right speech, and They surely will contact you. And when They contact you, you will not be devastated because Their contact will draw and expose whatever is filthy within your nature. Their presence also will help your inner potentials bloom.

Many people say, "That is my Master." This is another signal of rejection. If you know about your Master, you will be careful not to sell His name in the bazaars.

We must know that we do not choose our Master, but the Master chooses us when we are ready. From that moment on our lips are sealed from profane speech.

People occupied with their personality cannot fall under the searchlight of the Masters. They need people who live a soul life, a practical life illumined by the Soul light. It is this light which will bring the power of the Masters to the world and help humanity in its need.

Disciples will be those who are sensitive to Hierarchical impression and have certain experiences where, at times, they knew they were overshadowed by Them. If this experience is not there, and they are victims of other leads, the work cannot go on the right lines. A disciple is sensitive to the Hierarchical lead, and all that he wants to do is his Master's will, Who may overshadow him at certain times to make his service more effective. The more the disciple empties his ego, vanity, and personality, the more useful an agent he can be in the hands of the Masters. His individuality radiates the power of his Master and radiates his own words and power because he stands in the consciousness of his Master.

Very often a disciple has a very long series of sacrifices, self-abnegation, and heroism from the past. They accumulate and make him chooseable. This past collection of living deeds, service, and self-renunciation eventually brings him to the presence of his Master. The more such disciples stand in front of the Master, the more the world salvation will follow in its right path.

5

CONTEMPORARY MASTERS

To each Light-bearer, special duties are assigned. What each one did cannot be compared with what the others did. Their works can only be related and fitted to each other as if one were weaving a precious tapestry. One is not better than the other.

It is also not goal-fitting to try to find fault in the literature of various Light-bearers. It was given at different times to meet the needs of the prevailing conditions. If, indeed, there are differences, the student must try to see and develop his discrimination and make efforts to synthesize those differences.

For example, such a contemporary Light-bearer as H.P. Blavatsky brought the Teaching of schemes, chains, globes, and races. She tried to destroy the crystallization between religions and between religion and science and opened the door to the treasuries of ancient cultures. She gave a unique insight about the meaning of the Teachings of Great Ones. She laid a great foundation.

Helena Roerich gave the Agni Yoga Teaching, the Teaching of how to live as fiery beings, how to strive toward the future, how the whole existence is an integrated mechanism under the leadership of a Divine Presence. She gave the Teaching about psychic energy, imperil, fiery worlds, the Subtle World, the Cosmic Magnet, universal liberation for women, and spoke about the most essential subjects.

Alice Bailey gave the precious Teaching on chakras, the etheric body, the Antahkarana, the Chalice, the nature of the seven Rays, initiation, and discipleship. This Teaching synthesized the teachings of H.P. Blavatsky and Helena Roerich.

Alice Bailey also gave us three other aspects of the Teaching:

— Triangles to promote goodwill

— The World Invocation

— The New Group of World Servers

Actually, Alice Bailey's duty was to demystify the work of Blavatsky which most of the time was inaccessible to the average reader.

These three women's works, if read carefully, are one unit. Their intention and goal was to

- create the brotherhood of humanity
- bring freedom
- bring achievements and spiritual attainment
- put people in contact with the Divine potentials in their spirit
- reveal the Hierarchy
- reveal the Plan
- reveal the purpose of life
- create cooperation between all races and nations
- bring economic stability

The leaders of the world are impelled to reach the standards which were put before humanity by these three women serving the Hierarchy.

The enemies of mankind are many. They attack those energy formations which are destined to change human life and bring universal cooperation and unity and establish contact with the Higher Worlds. The intention of the enemies of humanity is to hate Beauty, Goodness, Righteousness, Joy, Freedom, and the unity which these great servants of Light tried to bring into the world. Hence, the enemies organize various attacks upon the sources of the Teaching.

It is very interesting that such attackers of the Teaching, first of all, do not read the Teaching in depth but reflect the ideas of spiritually blind people. Instead of attacking the Teaching, they should discuss the problems of

▲ pollution

▲ degeneration of morality

▲ widespread corruption

▲ violence

▲ murder

▲ drugs

▲ prostitution

▲ perversion

▲ corruption in governments

▲ separativeness

▲ hatred

They are prevalent everywhere. Their main target is to destroy the sources which are feeding people with Light, Love, Beauty, and right human relations.

There is also a dispute about who from the Hierarchy will come as the new Messiah. The Hierarchy is not composed of personalities. It is one unit. Whoever comes from the Hierarchy is the Hierarchy because the coming new Messiah is going to give the message of the Hierarchy.

When the Great Teacher speaks about the Christ, He said it is the name of an office, not of a person. It is pitiful that the reappearance of the coming One becomes an intellectual game to support special interests.

Actually, Whoever comes is bringing the message of Light, Love, and Willpower. Hierarchy can delegate only one in the name of the Purpose of the Lord of Shamballa.

Let us not act as theologians but speak more inclusively.

Within the enemies of mankind you can find those who read the Teaching given by these great servants. Charged with the Teaching, they exercise criminal attacks upon the Teaching, calling it by many names, trying to sow seeds of doubt, cleavages, and eventually hatred in the hearts of those who study the Teaching.

The new day cannot come by dishonoring and belittling the Great Workers who, throughout ages, by their own means and ways, tried to bring Light, Love, and Beauty to humanity.

It is impossible to create a superior civilization and culture while crushing under your feet the flowers of beauty that have blossomed throughout all ages as messengers of Light and glory. The servants of wisdom respect and worship every diamond given by all religions, sciences, and arts.

New generations are more intuitive than we think. Their consciousness strives toward unity, and wherever they see a labor to create cleavages, they withdraw. Wherever there is synthesis, they give their assistance. It is very ugly to raise the reputation of a Great One upon the ruination of another Great One.

Those who really have contact with the Hierarchy cannot pursue self-interest, individual honor and glory by belittling Teachers and the Teachings of various ages.

Those who really have contact with the Hierarchy seek unity, sacrifice their vanity and glamors, and especially sacrifice their judgment originating from their self-interest and lower mechanical mind.

People try to compare the labor of Buddha, Krishna, Moses, Christ, Mohammet and reach conclusions that one of them is better than the other. They even try to create hatred against the work of this or that Great One. This brings in moral degeneration, wrecking the spirit of devotion, dedication, and striving in all nations.

The work of these Great Ones is not given for academic study but for self-transformation. Their Teachings can be only understood through actualization and attainment, not by theological, dogmatic exercises.

On the trees of all Great Ones you can see the most precious flowers and fruits of attainments.

Attacking one of Them is actually attacking all of Them because Their message is one which was given to meet the need of different ages and different conditions. Rejecting the message of one, you reject the message given by all.

Workers in the field of Light, can betray their own teaching when they engage themselves in belittling any teaching given for the transformation of humanity.

For many ages zealots of this or that teaching burned and destroyed the books of other teachers trying to raise the reputation of the Teacher they were attracted to. Such events are still repeating themselves in the form of fires prepared by those who have keen intellect but no spirit.

In the coming days, not only "book burning" but also criticism based on hatred and self-interest will be concentrated in other forms of burning. This is what Christ was trying to say when He spoke about not working against the Holy Spirit, against the essence of unity, the spirit of unity, existing consciously in all those who are dedicated to helping humanity.

Actually, if you study the works of these three great women, you will see that they were concerned with the vision of the new world. Their message can only be understood by using each of their teachings as a key to interpret and touch the essence of the other.

One day I told my Teacher that I can understand the message of Christ better after studying intensely the messages of Krishna and Buddha. My Teacher looking into my eyes said, "Now you found the key, do not lose it. . . ."

It is a great mistake if a worker creates any cleavage in the construction of the Teaching. But it is a grave and unpardonable sin if any messenger tries to create any cleavage in the Temple of the Teaching or between the Teachers of Light.

6

MASTERS AND LABOR

Those who work in the Hierarchy are free in Their labor. Every one works in His or Her specialization for the future. Every one tries to take His experiments to the highest.

Hierarchical members are not omniscient. They are on the path of expanding Their consciousness. They are expanding, experiencing, and expressing.

All discoveries help the overall knowledge of the Hierarchy. They welcome every knowledge that is the result of experiment. All that is going on in the membership of the Ashram is fundamentally scientific.

Every one is free to carry His or Her experience. There is no higher and lower knowledge. All Their knowledge is revelation of knowledge and of the Laws of Cosmos.

This means that Masters are researchers and workers. They are not those people Who know everything, Who can do everything, and Who are everything. On the contrary, They are great toilers. Of course, Their consciousness is far more expanded than ours. We are sometimes ants in comparison to Them, but also They are babies in comparison to the Cosmic awareness.

The Hierarchy is in constant change, constant adjustment, and constant striving.

Year after year the Hierarchy changes, improves, or readjusts Its plans and working procedures to keep pace with human development and with the changing energies which pour into our planet. In addition, the expansion of the Masters' consciousness exercises pressure on the way Hierarchy should work in the future.

Hierarchical people are like the executives in our corporations. For example, executives not only try to benefit from every invention but also from every opportunity to put the corporation at the top, especially with regard to equipment and personnel. Hierarchy, too, is a hundred times more progressive than our corporations. They benefit from higher ideas, revelations, and energies made available to Them and also by the need presented by advancing humanity.

We are told that cyclically the Hierarchy improves Their plan and the application of Their ideas, readjusting themselves to spatial energies. This helps us to understand that the inner group of Masters is not stuck with antiquities but is eager to grasp every opportunity to serve humanity with the highest efficiency possible.

In the Hierarchy every single member is charged with enthusiasm, with future, and with endless service. Their service extends toward the seven fields of human labor. For each field there is a special Ashram. Ashrams are specialized fields to meet each field of human endeavor.

The highest executives in any field receive ideas and visions from their corresponding Ashram. If this tie is pure and strong, the executive becomes a fiery part of labor and inspiration in his field.

The Hierarchy has many agents in every field of human labor. That is why we can see a steady march toward progress, toward the new. Each field is approaching other fields for co-operation and greater service.

The source of expansion of all fields is the expansion of the Hierarchy. Expansion of the Hierarchy is like a tremendous pressure making the human machine go forward and upward.

There is an opinion that holy people, saints, teachers, gurus, and Masters retire after they die or that they go to heaven and paradise to rest or to enjoy divine beauties. This is not the case. Every advancing and responsible person, at whatever stage of life, engages himself in hard work, in hard labor on behalf of humanity, and periodically keeps pace with changing spatial energies and human need.

The whole of Hierarchy thinks about how best to save humanity and meet its needs.

7

MASTERS AND STRIVING

Masters, in whatever form They are presented, inspire striving. The more realistic the presentation, the deeper effect it has on our consciousness. One thing we must remember is that Masters were once human with all human weaknesses and powers. The only power that raised Them to a superhuman level was striving toward perfection. Striving creates a kind of power, which in turn feeds the striving.

In all Their life, Masters characterized genuine, sincere, real striving. Striving was Their wings, Their power, Their joy. No one can raise above himself without striving. Striving is the energy of that dynamic core which is the inheritance of every traveler on the path. This fuel perpetually keeps the torch of striving burning and moves us to eternal heights of beingness.

Masters, for us, are the symbol of progressive striving. No one can respect his Master or become His disciple unless he strives toward perfection. The endlessness of the path is the source of Their enthusiasm. Nothing strongly inspires Them but the image of perfection, and this image always moves ahead as They approach it.

Once you enter onto the path of striving, many riddles of life become simple facts. Striving expands your consciousness and elevates your consciousness and your position. You can see and experience on the level of perpetual progress.

A Master stands out as an image of worship, as an image of devotion, as an inspiring presence for your striving toward perfection.

Christ gave the plan for humanity. The plan for humanity is "to be perfect as your Father in Heaven is perfect." There is no other plan. Each plan that humanity can create must have this dynamic nucleus. If this dynamic nucleus exists in every plan humanity conceives, then the world will go toward glory and more glory.

Many people think that Masters do not need to improve Themselves, that They are already perfect. Such opinions have no foundation. Not only do Masters move toward perfection but also all creation, all superior spirits, angels, and devas move toward perfection.

Striving is the law of the Universe. Disobeying this law degenerates people, groups, and nations. Every step taken in the Cosmic law brings a current of life. Eventually, we understand that striving toward perfection is the entrance to life. Life is assimilated by the power of striving. Without striving, life ceases to be.

The stronger one becomes in life, the deeper he dives into the currents of striving. Masters are road signs on the path of striving.

8

MASTERS AND JOY

The Masters are sources of joy and the Hierarchy is the vortex of joy. Nothing can take away the joy of a Master because He is under the currents of bliss from Shamballa.

Those of us who have made a contact with a true Master can feel His joy for many years, and it turns into the energy of striving and sacrificial service in us.

Without contact with the Hierarchy, life turns into a burden even with all our wealth and power. It is joy that gives meaning to all our actions because it leads to the Hierarchy.

In immense difficulties, barriers, and hindrances, joy opens the way and paves the path of ascent. Without Hierarchy a person is an abandoned orphan.

It is time now to organize groups everywhere who are of one accord and who strive, meditate, and serve to spread the energy of the Hierarchy. Wherever there are three, four, seven, nine disciples gathered together to contact the Hierarchy and spread the energy of the Hierarchy, they render a great service to humanity and to the Hierarchy. But these groups must realize from the beginning that they exist to transmit the influence of the Hierarchy to the world.

These groups must live in the consciousness of the Hierarchy and feel that they are thinking, feeling, and acting in the spirit and love and light of the Hierarchy.

Such groups do not stand for any ideology or religion. Their interest is to bring love and goodwill to humanity so that humanity uses groups to create a life on the planet which will inspire others to strive toward perfection and synthesis.

The Hierarchy stands as a source of energy and guidance. Those who gather together in the name of the Hierarchy will receive Hierarchical energy and guidance, which will make them magnetic and radioactive centers in humanity. Without this, some people will have neither a purpose nor a direction in life. Without purpose and direction, a lost life is on the arc of decline and destruction.

Ashrams, and the totality of Ashrams which is the Hierarchy, are a vortex of joy. All of the Masters sing joyful songs while working. All relationship is based on joy. Joy is the atmosphere of the Hierarchy in which Masters labor.

From where does this joy originate? From the awareness of service. As They serve, joy flows out of Them and spreads to all corners of the Hierarchical location. It even penetrates flowers, bushes, and trees and goes to the earth, to the disciples tuned-in with Them.

In joy Their efforts are multidimensional. Their destination is clear, the hindrances disappear, and all the atmosphere is charged with electromagnetic energies.

No one can enter the Hierarchy except through joy. No one can labor there except with joy because joy is the sign of purity and mastery. Joy is the sign of ever-givingness, renunciation, and living in beingness.

The Great Sage says, "If once you hear our singing in the Brotherhood. . . ." Singing in its essence is elimination of all friction and the establishment of all harmony, cooperation, and oneness.

Hierarchy performs a multidimensional labor to meet the multidimensional needs of humanity, but in this labor there is not a single ripple which creates disharmony. All labor flows like a joyful song in utmost harmony and perfection.

One may ask: What if Their labor is rejected by people or distorted? Do They feel upset? Their labor does not have anticipation. They labor for the need, and They know that over time it will be assimilated. Hierarchical labor is never lost. Place and time differ, but the jewels find their proper soil, even if They are rejected by the one to whom help was directed.

Distortion of Their help is also considered. And They know that once Their help reaches a person, it will grow as an energy, eventually conquering the person's weakness.

Joy circulates among Them like a river of energy. Their heart and spirit manifest joy every moment, especially when they are under heavy tension.

They think in joy; They communicate through joy; They greet each other in joy. Joy keeps all the atmosphere of the Hierarchy pure and electromagnetically tense.

People can contact Them if they develop joy — a joy that is real, sacrificial, radioactive. Such a joy attracts Their attention. All true servers are collected under Their wings by joy.

Whoever was able to be a part of any Ashram and had a chance to visit the Hierarchy, you see his face glowing with joy. He turns into a dispenser or an agent of joy. And joy creates that magnetism which draws people into joy. This is how real groups are formed. Each member is attracted not by an outer Teaching but by the joy of the group.

9

―――――― ❦ ――――――

MASTERS AND PROTECTION

Many people, when they start meditating and reading Hierarchical literature, are apt to think that they are now in the
Master's aura, and He will protect them from many evils.
Even some students are grieved and angry seeing that their
life is not happy or smooth, but that they are passing on a
bumpy road with many pains and suffering. They occasionally
blame their supposed Master, and think that He is failing to
give them a pleasant life, comforts, and so on.

First of all, your life is the life of your karma. Your life is
the manifestation of your past karma. A Master never inter-
feres with the Law of Karma. The Law of Karma is very sacred
to Them, and They allow you to confront your karma.

If you are dedicated to the cause of the Hierarchical Plan,
Masters have the right to interfere in your life events only when
these events are not the result of your karma, but are the result
of psychic attacks or attacks that come from dark forces.[1]
When this is the cause, They may interfere. Sometimes, even

―――――――――――――

1. See *Battling Dark Forces*, Ch. 2.

in these cases, They want you to handle your problem without Their assistance, so that you strengthen yourself and make yourself ready to fight the negative forces in Nature — psychic attacks, subconscious attacks, and so on.

In rare cases, when you exhaust your energies and an attack is heavy, They interfere and smash the attack and free you in order to prepare you to become a greater warrior.

Their whole intention is to make you stand on your feet and face your karma or fight against attacks.

It is very difficult to discriminate between attacks and karma, but the Masters know this, and They extend Their hand if you are under attack. Also, you will begin to know the difference between attacks and karma and prepare yourself to confront them.

Sometimes they are very obvious. You are condemned for a crime that you did not commit. If it happens that you are really sentenced for something you did not do, in the next life you receive your compensation. Righteousness is the law of the Higher Worlds, and Masters work under the Law of Righteousness.

When you work hard and gradually gain Their confidence and reach higher stages of discipleship, They will protect you from any attack automatically.

To reach to this stage is not easy. Life after life we are in the training process. We learn and experiment and experience. The major attitude of the disciple is to focus his dedication on His Master without expectation whatsoever but with firm faith that He is watching you.

10

MASTERS AND THEIR TRAINING

Often we are asked whether the Masters go through periods of training and why. They go through training in many ways to perfect Their receptivity and world service.

Receptivity is related to a higher center in the planet which holds vaster secrets about the purpose of Planetary life, Solar life and Cosmic life. Advanced Hierarchical members receive Their direction, orientation, and labor to transmit to those who are functioning in the field of world service to inspire them, to encourage them, and to keep them in line with the Higher Will.

Their training is related to registering clearly the Source and the message of the Higher Will, to understand and assimilate it, and to be able to appropriate it for those who are in the battlefield of world events.

They need to unfold and synchronize Their higher centers and senses, build the higher parts of the Antahkarana from Atmic and Monadic to Divine. They need to develop courage and strength to stand in contact with Higher Lives with exactitude and to pass Their impressions to those who serve.

Those Masters Who are turning Their attention to world

events and serving people to help solve crucial problems undergo different training, for example:

- how to appropriate Their vehicles into the atmosphere of human emanations
- to know the principle active in the seven fields of human labor
- to discover the fields which are more appropriate in making a contact with humanity
- to find advanced disciples and initiates and inspire them to be points of light in their field
- to see the karmic consequences and to correct Their approach accordingly
- to handle those nations which are open to the Hierarchical Plan
- to train workers in the heroic work of world salvation

There is another phase to Their training: how to be unaffected by evil personified and to see the issues as they are and how to see the good in humanity without being caught up in humanity's maya, glamors, and illusions. This study may take hundreds of years to master and to put into use.

A Master is one Who takes the responsibility to go forward and to benefit humanity with all His achievements.

We are told that They do not miss time or opportunity to train Themselves to render service.

They are world scientists, and They develop Themselves in scientific thoroughness because They are handling fire and They are working with fire. This means that the smallest mistake made by Them can have cataclysmic consequences.

In a nation, especially in higher levels, every center, every combination, every cycle, every current of energy changes. There are also energies which can be poisonous for our planet, energies that are far beyond our capacity to assimilate. They watch all these and many other points for the safety of human evolution. "Sometimes," says the Great Sage, "Our sweat, like a drop of blood, falls from Our forehead."

We must remember, in fact, that the planet, solar system, Cosmos, the galaxy, the Universe are fields of training. Every Spark of life strives toward perfection to serve intelligently and wisely, and the Master on that path is a few thousand miles ahead of us.

HIERARCHICAL TRAINING   *Astrology ?*

In the Hierarchy there is a group whose duty it is to study the relationship of the celestial bodies, the relationship of energies, their interchange, and the chemistry they create. They study to find out the cycles, the critical moments, the opportunities in order to protect humanity or to aid humanity. They are great naturalists, and Nature teaches Them how to benefit from the changes, cycles, and shifts.

They present Their observations to the Hierarchy, and Hierarchy mobilizes all Its forces to create a network through which benevolent energies can be directed to humanity. Prominent disciples act as the distributing points for these energies. *Me holding down a corner of the energy tent!*

Hierarchical members are not omnipotent people. They are the adult children of Nature and celestial bodies. They learn the laws of Cosmos every moment. They try to help humanity in its struggle for life.

People make Masters to be gods. Indeed, They are very advanced in comparison to human beings, but in comparison to the Universe They may be humble students. Their mastery over themselves does not mean total mastery of the Universe. It is the result of Their past experiences, knowledge, service, and sacrifice, but new and wider horizons are waiting for Them to proceed toward relative perfection.

Everything They learn from celestial bodies They share with the members of the Hierarchy. The Hierarchy, in turn, decides how to use this information for Their service to humanity and Their advance toward Shamballa.

Most of the members of the Hierarchy are from humanity. They are clearly familiar with the cause of our suffering, karma, and ignorance. They have great compassion for us, and They try to stimulate our striving in order that we may proceed on the path of perfection.

If new energies are available in Cosmos, They try to bring them to our planet and, using certain methods, distribute the energies among humanity to prevent inertia, hatred, fear, paralysis and to impress cooperation, harmony, and understanding.

At certain times They are forced to perform surgery in humanity in the form of cataclysms, then protect the rest of the world from Cosmic shocks.

There are Existences and Beings in Kosmos in relation to which our great Masters stand as ants. This is how the whole Existence is — the Mystery of Mysteries. We have gratitude to the Masters and Hierarchy Who established a station for the progress of humanity and for the study of the great Kosmos.

11

MASTERS AND HIERARCHY

Hierarchy is not the collective body of ghosts, astral entities, or those entities that come to mediums and talk through them. Hierarchy is the living Headquarters of a World Educational Group.

The group is formed by all Teachers of all religions. They are very Great Ones. They started like us, as human beings, and then developed, stage by stage, into higher levels of consciousness. They mastered Their lives, Their personalities, Their minds, Their bodies, and became perfect on all planes.

Most of Them live in the world. They have bodies like us. Some of Them have bodies which are etherically composed. Some can materialize and look like we do. Some of Them are working on the physical plane. Some of Them are working on the mental plane and higher spheres, but all of Them are closely connected and telepathically in contact with each other. They watch everything going on in this world.

A Great One says that we have in the Hierarchy a mechanism, a computer, that immediately registers if someone announces the word of Hierarchy. For example, there was a

71

disciple who was in danger. Suddenly, he heard his Master's voice, "Don't walk anymore. Stop there!" The disciple was saved from a great danger. His Master was a thousand miles away.

We are going to be like Them. Our brain has so many secrets in it. Humanity is using only two or three percent of its brain. If the centers of the brain are developed and unfolded, we will have a television within us which has all channels. Anytime we want to key in with any event, with any person, we will see in our eyes what is going on all over the world. In Hierarchical language that is called the mirror. Great Ones have Their mirrors. For example, in Hierarchy there is a big cave. On the walls of the cave there exist little images of all advancing disciples who are making new breakthroughs. A Great One, a member of the Hierarchy, comes and watches the images and, according to their color and radiation and intensity of vibration, recognizes immediately what is going on in the disciple.

Every moment They can watch you. They can see you. They can really understand you. A member of the Hierarchy will never interfere with your personal affairs. There is a very distorted and misleading idea about Them. In some literature it says that the Masters are involved with us, with whom we must marry, what we must eat, what job we must do, which girlfriend we must choose, this or that. In reality, They are not interested at all. They are only interested in global progress, advancement, and transformation.

Those "Masters" whom you find in some literature are pseudo-masters, just fabrications of the human imagination. Real Ones deal with groups or masses. What do They do? They create mental and spiritual conditions and challenge us to strive toward Them. They do not force us. They do not violate our free will. They never impose Their ideas upon us. They just shine with Their beauty, with Their intellectual and spiritual mastery. They create and evoke within us some kind of striving toward Them, so that eventually we, as small seeds, become a big tree and reach our destination. We are just like acorns. There is a big, huge, oak tree which is our destination. That is a Master, a member of Hierarchy. What are we? We are seedlings yet. But our destination is very great. Our destination is to become like Them. That is why Christ once said, "Be perfect as your Father in Heaven is perfect."

He said something else that was very disturbing for some narrow-minded people. He said, "You will do greater things than I have done." The perfection of the Christ is not a barrier to our progress.

For example, you become a medical doctor of such high standard that no one can pass you. On the contrary, Hierarchical members have one rule: to create conditions that enable people around Them to surpass Them. This is never understood. We have an intention to keep people below us. We say, "Stop there, now. You are advancing too much. You should not go beyond me." The Hierarchical rule, which is totally the reverse, says that if you want to advance on the steps of universal perfection, make somebody advance more than you. This destroys your vanity, your ego, your jealousy, your stupidity, your narrow-mindedness. The teachers and leaders should not stand as a standard for, or as a barrier to, the pro-gress of other people.

When you go to the government, to big factories, to big organizations, you find one thing — those who are strong keep the weak ones back. "Just stay there. Do not advance beyond us." Even if a person is a genius, they want to destroy that genius so that he does not take their position. We know that. But in the Hierarchy the rule is totally different. What is the rule in the Hierarchy? If you want to advance on the path of Infinity, toward the perfection of God, you must make everyone more advanced than you are, so that eventually someone graduates to take your position and frees you to work in more responsible positions.

That was the secret which Christ revealed when He said, "The greatest among you must be the servant of all." We never understood this. Read books, watch television, read your newspapers, and you will see one thing — me, me, me — ours, ours, ours. That is what is keeping the world backward.

In the rule of Hierarchy, every Great One works to make somebody advance as fast as he or she can, without imposition. The Hierarchy is composed of many Great Ones from all religions: great saints, great masters of literature, art, philosophy, politics, and education. When people write about the Hierarchy, they give the impression that Hierarchical members are all religious people such as Christians, Buddhists, or Moslems. They are not. They belong to the whole. They do not have any "ism," any color, any belongings, here or there. World universality is in Their soul. They are universal.

They deal with you within the concept of universal achievements. If you are good, you are good because you think about the whole of humanity. If you are going to advance, you must develop the same spirit of universality. All of these people, from all races, all religions in the Hierarchy, compose the *cloud of witness*. The cloud of witness is the light that shines on the planet to educate humanity.

Energy Ten

How are we going to be educated if we do not have Teachers? We are told that many millions of years ago Great Ones came to infant humanity to teach them. They came from another planet and incarnated on this planet. They became the Kings and Queens and Teachers of humanity. How did They get started? They started with dances, dramas, recitations, chanting, discipline, education and slowly, slowly, They energized the fire in humanity. This was done in such a way that we are now developing in many dimensions. Behind all progress in humanity you will find a Master, a Great One,

Who inspires humanity.

In governments many Great Ones came and appeared and talked about something, and then disappeared. You do not hear about these happenings, because if the governments wrote about them humanity would say, "They are hallucinating. They are mediums. They are channels." However, you can find these kinds of events if you study very carefully the histories of many, many nations.

For example, in the Far East, the great Mongol emperor, King Akbar, was continuously in contact with Hierarchy. Once he was hunting, and his party surrounded many deer and wild animals. This large party of people intended to kill the animals. Suddenly the voice of Akbar's Master came. He said, "Meet Me under that tree." What they conversed about was not written down, but when Akbar came back he said, "We are not going to kill animals anymore."

The hunting party dispersed. They said, "We were ready to kill all of these animals." "You know, they are treasures," King Akbar said. "We will stop killing them." From that date on he made many changes in the palace and in the government. He was so benevolent, so beautiful. One thing that he did, and no king or president in the world has ever done this, was to collect all kinds of religious people and philosophers in his court. He had them talk about their religion and philosophy, and he listened. After two or three hours of listening he would say, "You know, some of you are right. Some of you do not know what you are talking about." Then he wanted to see all religions united, because he saw that the Hierarchy was composed not from one religion but from all religions.

You can find this story and information in the Sufi literature in Central Asia, where there are great Sufi Masters, very Great Ones. Some people think They are heathens, but if you ever saw two or three of Them, you would be surprised. They are powerful individuals, holy, beautiful, magnetic.

One day we were at school in the Far East. The Teacher said, "Today a guest is coming." Before the guest arrived we started to shiver. We had already attracted a Great One's energy. He came and talked for half an hour. We were in heaven! Such Great Ones are in every religion and from every nationality.

The members of the Hierarchy will walk among us. There will be no mine and yours, my religion, my race, my nationality, my country, but there will be a real united symphony of the cream of humanity,

In history we read that most of these great members of the Hierarchy Who came to the world and gave a higher teaching to us were born from the same mother. For example, the Mother of Mercury and Hermes was called Maya. The Mother of Siamus was called Savior. The Mother of Samanakadem was called Maya. The Mother of Adonis was called Mira. The Mother of Buddha was called Maya. The Mother of Christ was called Mary.

Now look what is happening to the members of the Hierarchy. They belong to all religions. First of all, when we speak about Christ in a Christian way, we say Christ belongs to Christianity. Christ is not even a Christian. Christianity was formed later. Of course you will be shocked reading this. Christ never wanted to establish a religion. He had only one religion, which was "love each other as I love you." Create right human relations, peace on earth, and glory to God. That is His philosophy or religion.

If we keep the simplicity of Christ, how He lived, how He cared for everyone, how He was crucified and suffered for us, we will not speak about preaching and giving sermons. We will love and help each other.

The members of the Hierarchy were all like us. Eventually some of Them built Their soul. People all over the world think that they are immortal human beings. You will never be immortal until you reach immortality through your

76

Kingdom of God = Immortality

own striving, labor, sacrifice, service, and by being a soul.

If you read advanced esoteric literature, you will see that millions and millions of humans perish after they die because they did not build the immortal principle within themselves, which we call soul. In order to become immortal, it is necessary to have a connection with your higher principles so that when you die, you are not obliterated and annihilated, but instead you are conscious of the infinite path.[1]

All members of the Hierarchy demonstrate a life of sacrificial service. All of Them render sacrificial and dedicated service to humanity, not to Their nation only, but to all humanity. They render service to the planet, to the trees, to the rivers and lakes, to the animals, to the angels. Sivananda · Love all, serve all

All of Them speak and challenge us to become immortal. None of Them said that there is no life after death. Their main topic was to urge you to prepare yourself for immortality. When They asked Christ, "How can we reach immortality?" (which was the Kingdom of God symbolically), He said, "You can take the Kingdom of God, or immortality, by violence." What is violence? Violence is heavy labor and striving.

Study, meditate, work, sacrifice, labor. You are going to work to change yourself. Unless you work and change yourself, you are going to be like a dry leaf that the wind will come and blow away.

Did you ever sit down and think what is going to happen to you after you die? You may think angels are waiting to lead you like a queen or king into heaven. You just dream about it! Nobody is waiting for you! Think about what is going to happen to you after you pass away. Prepare yourself and search.

I knew a man who was very rich and powerful. Suddenly one day he came to the school. I was the headmaster of the school. The man said, "I came to hug you, to kiss you, and to tell you good-bye. For fifty-five years I worked for my body,

---

1. See *The Psyche and Psychism.*

for my dollars, for building, selling, trading. I am with women, with this, with that, but I suddenly remembered that very soon I am going to die. I am going to prepare myself."

I said, "Really!" He said, "Yes, I am going to a cave in the mountains. If you want to visit sometime, it will be fine with me." I was so emotional, because I loved him very much. He was also a great Teacher.

He disappeared. Four years later I said, "You know, I would like to visit that man." I got a horse and rode and rode. I found him living in a cave. The whole cave was in light. I said, "Teacher, what is this light?" "I do not know," he said. Many years later he passed away. We did not know anything more about him.

I am not telling you to leave your bank accounts and properties and businesses to work out your salvation. You do anything you want, but this is what my Teacher did.

Most of the members of the Hierarchy were born from Virgins. Is this an hallucination? Can a Virgin bring forth a child? One day a friend of mine was getting married. Somebody came to take me to the wedding so that I could bless their marriage. As we were traveling, the driver said, "I have a question that I know you will not be able to answer." He asked, "Do you have proof that Christ was born from a Virgin?"

I answered, "First of all, it does not matter, but I have a question for you. If you answer my question, I will answer your question." He said, "What is it?" "Well," I said, "suppose you have two gods. One god is able to make a Virgin have a child. The other god is not able to make a Virgin have a child. Which god will you worship?"

"Well," he said, "do not ask anymore. You got me." He was stuck. If he had said, for example, that God cannot do anything, he would have contradicted his idea about God.

"Do you see?" I said, "God can do anything."

Is that not beautiful? Most of the Great Ones were born from Virgin girls. It could not be otherwise because the mother's body must be so pure. You cannot have a very high-level Initiate and Master born from a woman who had been with three hundred men. Physically, emotionally, mentally, it is impossible. That is why purity is so important.

All of the Great Ones passed through intense suffering. Most of them were crucified, stoned, killed, buried alive, or their heads and hands were cut off. This was the public's reaction to their beauty and purity, which humanity could not digest or accept.

It is so interesting that all of Them emphasized two things: forgiveness and absolute love, not revenge and hatred, anger and destruction. None of Them said that. All Their actions were motivated by love, gratitude, and forgiveness.

There were many names of Great Ones born of Virgins. Isis of Egypt was born from a Virgin. It is in the books. There was Christ in Bethlehem; Krishna, the same thing. There is Maeletta, Tamus, Mercury, Aesopolus, Basshus, Hercules, Pisceus, Dionysius, Mitra, Zoroaster, Buddha, Confucius, Lao Tse, Hiawatha, Dekanawidah, Canus in Assyria, Astrad in Syria. All were born from Virgins. I was told when I was in Asia that even many mothers of Sufi Masters never married.

All these Great Ones, saints, and great Masters are from all religions and all departments of human endeavor. Masters are sometimes great politicians, great kings, great presidents, and great educators, not only religious people.

They are great philosophers. For example, in England, we are told that there are two great Masters Who are philosophers. In North America, we have two great Ones Who work on the mental plane inspiring the American public with some kind of philosophical, mystical thinking. You can see the results from what is happening.

We also have great Masters of art. The Great Sage, talking

about the Hierarchy says, "If one day you have the readiness to visit our Ashram you will see the great pieces of art, scientific research, and so on." Suppose I created some sculpture, a very beautiful masterpiece, which is in the Hierarchy now. One thousand years later when I become a Master, I could go and look at it and say, "Wow, look what I created in the past."

Great painters are there. Great scientists are there. For example, before any scientific invention is given to humanity, it is tested in the Hierarchy. They have mathematicians and scientists, the highest that humanity can produce. That is our destination. That is my destination. We are going to go there. That is the school that will lead to the solar school later.

They are also great religious leaders from all religions. They are also great financiers. See how beautiful it is! What is finance and economy? It is the power, the ability to organize materialized energy in such a way that we create a paradise on this earth. If you saw our banking system from two hundred years ago compared to now, you would see tremendous advancement. How did this advancement start? It started by the inspiration of the Hierarchy.

It started by educating people, by causing changes so that humanity advances not only in religion but also in all phases of life. Physically, you must advance. Emotionally, mentally, spiritually, you must advance. You must not only have money, properties, and peace of mind but also must be a scientist. You must pray, be an artist, be a leader, understand politics, so that you, as a diamond, polish all facets of your diamond. This is how we can reach perfection.

The idea of Hierarchy is not narrow. It is an all-synthesizing concept.

One day, somebody said, "Hierarchy does not exist." Why not? If a university exists, Hierarchy exists. What is a university? It is a station for those who finished high school. After you finish high school, where do you go if you want to proceed? You go to the university. After you finish the university, where do you go? To hell or to heaven!

Oh yes, many university students go to hell, but some of them go to heaven also. Is that not interesting?

People argue about the existence or nonexistence of Masters. People do not realize that things exist if you make them exist. Nothing exists before the moment you make them exist. Once they exist, they continue to exist.

Something stops existing if you fail to prove the existence of that something in your thoughts, feelings, and actions. As long as it exists in your thoughts, feelings, and actions, it never stops existing.

Actually there are things that are created by superior powers, and those things exist because the superior powers created them.

We must understand that nothing exists if you do not create it.

All angels and monsters exist because we created them. It is important to know if a creation makes you happy or unhappy. Some creations make people unhappy; others make us happy, but people debate about the existence or nonexistence of such creations.

The strongest creations are those which are brought into existence by the multitudes.

Some creations are mental, others are emotional, others physical. Some feel their mental creations, some the emotional, some the physical. Some people make a physical existence have an emotional or mental existence or vice versa.

Those existences which bring the most happiness to the largest number of people never die, but people attack them and then strengthen their existence. Any creation needs believers and non-believers. This is how an existence is tempered.

It is interesting to know that those who create something

are also those who can annihilate it. This is always true — one eventually becomes the enemy of his creations if he lacks the power to recreate it again and again or to regenerate it, to make it fit to new conditions.

For a baby, it is a tragedy to destroy his teddy bear as something that has no right to exist for an adult.

The majority of humanity are grownup children, especially if you see them fighting on battlefields. Their intention is to destroy each other's teddy bears.

To destroy their teddy bears one must replace them with greater toys, toys which give them more joy. People try to destroy things that are indestructible.

One day a man said to my Father, "Why do you love that Jesus Who never even existed." My Father answered, "Do you have something better for me to believe in?" The man fell silent, then answered, "I guess not," and departed without another word.

The most important factor is discrimination. One must create through discrimination and create those "realities" which will do good for people and nations.

Discoveries are not creations. They are processes of rediscovering things that existed in the past.

People think that God created all that exists. He created only those who could create. All those which exist are created by his creatures. God is thought to be Creator, Sustainer, and Destroyer. All this is true except that He was created by man when man needed to have a Creator.

Before man or intelligent beings existed, who could know the existence of God? That is why we say that gods were men, and men wanted to have God and so created God within himself.

All the stars are men turned into gods.

Masters are those Beings who created Themselves, and because They created Themselves They cannot stop existing.

Life purpose

It is to our advantage to accept Their existence, to learn how to recreate ourselves and become Masters.

It is interesting that some superior beings are created by very highly evolved Existences. These superior beings live, act, and do things totally by the remote control of these highly advanced Existences.

The meaning is simple. Any form created for the benefit of all continually becomes a source of blessings. Any form created from the self or separative interest becomes a source of pain and suffering for humanity for a long time.

Why reject Masters if They are the manifestation of Beauty, Goodness, Righteousness, Joy, Freedom, wisdom, and power? Is there any better form than the Masters Who are as real as your soul? Attacking Masters creates a world without principles, without purpose, without vision. Do not reject Them but search more about Them, and strive to be like Them.

Question: Do these Great Ones create the vision for Their birth?

Answer: You and I and many people live in the time concept. Time is a limiting factor in our minds. For the Great Ones, there is no beginning, there is no end, there is no time. They live in timelessness. So, for Them, the future and the past and the present are the same, but in our mind we cannot understand this concept because our brain limits our understanding.

They are Their own vision. They are Their own past. They are Their own future. The chicken and the egg — which came first?

They have three main labors.

1. *The first labor is to make humanity proceed on the way to perfection.* That is the main labor. They want everyone, from every race and religion to advance, to transform, to transfigure himself until he becomes love, light, and energy.

We are a great energy in this little body. When we develop

83

our energy side, the little body will radiate all that purity, beauty, and creativity. We must reach that stage. All Great Ones in every religion, the angels, and the prophets show us that this is possible. "Look, I did it," They say.

One day I read and re-read the *New Testament* so much that I said, "I do not want to read it anymore." I was in the forest where I lived alone. I did not know where to go. Suddenly I opened the little *New Testament* which my Mother put in my pocket. I put my finger on a passage and read what Christ said, "Be courageous, I overcame the world." "Oh," I said, "you know, I cannot leave you alone. I must read you again."

Be courageous. The work of Great Ones is to create courage in you so that you go home and say, "You know, I do not want to stay as I am." Once you start not liking yourself, you are stepping on the path of perfection. But if you are satisfied with your legs, your hair and think that everything is beautiful, you are going to be a stagnated lake, nothing else.

You are going to leave your image behind and seek a new image.[2] That is how you advance.

2. ***The second work of the Hierarchy is to prepare its members for Solar service.*** Planetary service is Their main labor, but for Solar labor, we are told, They go for special training. They work with major Rays and, with Their wisdom and power, purify the space as much as possible.

3. ***Their third work is to penetrate beyond the solar system*** and create cables of communication between advanced stars and galaxies and our planet so that we do not feel like we are an orphan in space.

Hierarchy is active on many planes, including our physical plane. They want us to live with the laws and principles of the Hierarchy which are given in every religion, in all education, in true philosophy. When we live according to these laws — the Laws of Light, Love, and Beauty — the Kingdom of

---

2. See *The Mystery of Self-Image.*

God will be externalized in the world and humanity will live in health, happiness, prosperity, and light. That is the aim of the Hierarchy for our humanity.

Question: Where are the members of the Hierarchy located?

Answer: Wherever you have a contact with Them, They are there. For us, we think in terms of location. They speak about space being Their home because They are in immediate communication. They are with each other even if They work in different locations on earth. They can see and hear each other any moment, anywhere.

The consciousness of the Higher Adepts has no location. This is a serious concept. Their consciousness functions in all the planes of the Cosmic Physical Plane, as if They were the planes. Non-locality is the characteristic of Their consciousness. They can live in the physical plane but act in the Intuitional Plane. They are always in contact with each other in all planes.

An Adept knows what His disciple is doing at any time, when the disciple thinks about Him, or when the disciple's mind gives Him a call.

Space and time vanish before a developing consciousness, and the consciousness merges into awareness.

Consciousness still has limitation in time and space, but awareness is beyond that because it is the property of the intuition and beyond.

THE LAW OF HIERARCHY

It seems to me that the Law of the Hierarchy is the Law of the Ladder. Ascension on a gradient scale leads to the Most High. Each step depends on the former steps and extends to the higher steps.

One grade receives from above and passes to below, receiving higher potentials and transmitting them to lower grades. Thus, as one goes higher on the ladder, he provides more powerful energy to the lower steps. Of course, as the energy descends to lower and lower steps, it is assimilated and qualified by the preceding steps.

Every one of us is on a ladder. We proceed upward. We pull upward those who are on the lower steps. Each time we proceed, we manifest a tremendous resourcefulness and creativity to lower levels. Thus, life continues receiving from higher steps and transmitting to the most basic steps, bound to each other by the Law of the Hierarchy.

On every step of the ladder we have some sort of creativity emanating from the higher step. Each step has different characteristics, different ways of translation of the Higher Will, but it is important to see in the phenomenon of life the operation of the Law of the Hierarchy in all these steps.

Every kingdom, every species is on its own specific step yet connected to each other, interrelated, spreading on its own level the highest impulse received from the highest level.

This whole life is interrelated in an orderly way from which we all benefit.

What about those links in the chain of the Hierarchy which are full of separatism, glamors, and illusions? Do they form the ladder of the Hierarchy? Their essence operates by the same law, but their personality does not. That is why the personality soon perishes, if the transformed consciousness does not control the personality. Karma helps in this process.

Each advancing soul on the ladder is an example for the lower level on how to proceed. Sometimes their examples of self-forgetfulness, harmlessness, and right speech are stable steps for the feet of those who follow them.

Sometimes their virtues are lamps on the path of followers. Sometimes their sacrificial nature is a great inspiration to those who struggle on lower levels.

The whole chain of evolution advances together by the

Law of the Hierarchy. Those who exercise ego, separatism, and totalitarianism are corpses on the ladder of evolution, and sooner or later they face their destiny.

The Law of the Hierarchy is the law of future, hope, striving. Once a person realizes that he is in the current of the Law of the Hierarchy, there is no waste of time for him. He gradually mobilizes those powers which uplift him and place him on the right rung of the chain. Once his consciousness accepts that he is in the chain, he lives a responsible life in order to receive from the higher and transmit to the lower the purest essence of what he receives.

In the Law of the Hierarchy man loses the will of his body, emotions, and mind, illusions, glamors, and maya and starts to be filled by the Higher Will which descends on him like a fiery, creative, magnetic current. He is now in the current, and he actualizes it in all his expressions.

Many people are struggling to find the higher step to hang onto. This higher step is often a teacher for whom they look. And once they find him, he becomes a link between them and a higher link. If they know how to deal with this teacher, they feel spiritual comfort because they find their place in life.

Actually these are not teachers, only higher links. Each teacher is a student of a higher link. We are told that even a Cosmic Logos is a student of a higher one, and so on. Imagine, we are pilgrims of Infinity. If we have teachers, they are the source of our spiritual life. But they are our teachers in a relative sense.

What a grateful feeling it is to have your teacher. You in turn become a teacher for the lower link, equipped with all that is necessary for transmission. To consciously enter into the Hierarchical chain and have responsibility to be active there is the greatest privilege you can have in life.

The Law of the Hierarchy enters into your soul and leads

you back toward the open ocean of Divine consciousness. The Hierarchy as a whole is progressive because the members respond to zodiacal cycles, solar cycles, Shamballic cycles, and human evolutionary cycles. A Master is one Who never stands on the same ground. He is always advancing and expanding. Every time He advances and expands, He breaks a vast area of crystallizations and limitations. This is the cause of human striving toward new horizons.

The progressiveness of the Hierarchy is not denial of old presentations of wisdom, but a search for new aspects of awareness and a translation of old formulations in new relationships, new viewpoints, which include greater territory in the consciousness.

Masters follow the Cosmic clock and try to find opportunities to help us. Every time the hand of the clock advances, They take new steps to be synchronous. Outdated factors are left behind to produce karma and be settled.

There is not a single object in the world which They ignore, and They try to present an object in a new way in accordance with new, expanding horizons. This is why when a group or organization is stuck in an "old age," Masters drop it after a few warnings. That organization becomes a hindrance for thousands of people for many years.

If you look at the groups which are on the way to disintegration, you will understand how Masters withdrew Their attention and, for a few hundred years, these groups became obstacles on the path of advancement. Not only did They withdraw Their attention from churches and other organizations but also from religions because the hardest thing for a religion is change. We have so many religions on the path of decay with social consequences.

Masters can help build new groups and new organizations if They have people who are keeping in step with the

Hierarchy.

The Hierarchy is an advancing light, whether humanity advances or not. They do Their best to help humanity, but if Their help is not assimilated, they leave humanity alone — which is the greatest disaster for humanity.

Sometimes They have extreme difficulty in presenting Themselves and Their instructions to humanity due to the limitation of Their mediators and disciples. It is very hard for Them to find those people who will transfer faithfully Their Teaching in purity, without mixing it with their illusions, glamors, habits, and personal views or various weaknesses.

Sometimes They take a big risk in choosing a mediator. If the mediator has served them in a few incarnations, and if he or she is keeping pace with the progress of the Hierarchy, They choose that person for a service. It is an honor and great glory to prepare oneself or one's children for future Hierarchical service.

They look for coworkers all over the world and use every opportunity to guide humanity, but sometimes They are greatly disappointed in those who do serve Them.

Not a single day passes that They do not expand Their consciousness toward new horizons. Many times in history They walked among men, but humanity did not appreciate such an honor. They will come again to show us the path of future attainment. We hope that many will be responsive to Them.

The legend says also that most of Them live in a place near the Himalayas. Some of Them live in different places, such as the Middle East, England, France, America, Russia, Brazil, Armenia, and in other locations. They travel around or labor in the same place. Their disciples need not be with Them in the same place. They contact and see them if necessary.

Most of Them live with Their consciousness in the Intuitional Plane where there is no time, no space, no location. As we expand our consciousness, we will be with Them forever.

Question: Do They have a name other than the Hierarchy?

Answer: Yes. They are also called the Christ and Triumphant Disciples. Those who conquer the "world" go to Them.

Question: What do They do?

Answer: They serve every need of humanity on all levels. One of Them wrote a letter to someone and said, "We work so much that sometimes our sweat falls down like drops of blood." The president of a great nation is the busiest and most responsible person. A Master's labor surpasses a president's labor one million times.

The Law of Hierarchy is the progressive advancement toward the Cosmic Magnet through associated bridges. The Law of the Hierarchy is to provide the progressive links leading to the highest, with each link following the will of the one who is on a higher level.

Hierarchy is based upon the Law of Succession. The Law of the Hierarchy is the remembrance of the leaders and the fulfillment of their visions.

Every organism or labor is founded upon the Law of the Hierarchy, upon the Law of Succession.

The Hierarchy is a chain of illuminated souls, with successively higher and greater lights, the top of which reaches the Most High.

The Hierarchy is a ladder on whose steps the elected souls travel toward the destiny of life. Without this bridge of Light no one can discover his Source. Every illuminated and achieved person forms part of one of the many links, and he himself becomes part of the path of the Hierarchy.

The principle of succession guides this path — more advanced and illuminated ones lead those who are left behind.

There is always a location for a person in the chain of the Hierarchy; that location or condition is used in order to aspire toward the higher links.

Every move toward the higher link provides an opportunity for lesser disciples to move ahead on the chain. The life in all links in the chain moves forward like a running current of light.

The whole story of achievement is acted out in the chain of the Hierarchy. No movement can be successful in life that is not based on the foundation and vision of the Hierarchy. It is the Law of the Hierarchy that creates integrity, alignment, inspiration, striving, harmony, cooperation, and an ever-deepening vision in the hearts of those who are part of the movement. This is why Sages never engaged in any labor before calling out the name of the Hierarchy.

The Hierarchy is called "the Great Service." No one can actually be a common part of the Hierarchy unless he has a long history of service throughout his many incarnations. Each cell in the body of the Hierarchy is a radioactive source of service on its own level and field of labor.

Each service is an effort to prepare people to enter into the links of the Hierarchy and move forward toward the Highest. The creative Source toward which the whole Hierarchy aspires is felt and realized as the members of the Hierarchy move forward.

Each system has its own Hierarchy, on the level on which that system exists, but all chains of the Hierarchies link with each other through their own Hierarch — the sun striving in their own system.

Each link of the Hierarchy and each chain of the Hierarchies reveal charges from the one creative Source, according to the intensity of their striving. It is the beam of striving that turns into a conductive network for the charges coming from the creative Source. This is true for every group who is inspired by the Hierarchy. Their strength is equal to their harmonious striving.

Entrance into the ranks of the Hierarchy develops in us the ability to contact the higher link. Without such a contact, we cannot have direction. It is right direction that enables us to make right decisions. With every right decision, we enable ourselves to assimilate the Fires of Space and fill our Chalice with the Treasures of Space. Thus, teach the Teaching of Fire.

Through understanding the Law of the Hierarchy, we begin to fulfill the Higher Will. Every person, every group, every nation that did not follow the Higher Will began to disintegrate. It is the fulfillment of the Higher Will that keeps living units integrated and moving toward the Highest.

Constructive activities are impossible without cooperating with the Hierarchy. A mighty constructive process is going on in the Existence. To take part in the might of the constructiveness, one must discover the chain of the Hierarchy. That is how one can become a builder. A builder is a coworker of the Hierarchy, and in each act of building he manifests the will of the higher link.

Masters cannot take revenge. When one becomes an Arhat, He takes a vow not to hurt any sentient being, not to take revenge. They change Their habitat frequently if They are living in cities so that people do not bother Them, show their animosity toward Them, and create reactions.

Although They are harmless, the Law protects Them highly. If anyone sends bad thoughts, feelings, or actions to Them, the waves of such attitudes go and hit Their aura and return to the sender with greater intensity.

The Law works for those who have pure auras, and the reaction is automatic. That is why They warn people not to engage in harmful actions against Them because They are protected by Law.

However, people persecute Them, ignoring the consequences. They even kill Them and burn Them but, in time, the tidal wave comes and destroys their foundation altogether. Even nations sometimes fall into such destruction by hurting Those Who are dedicated to the highest.

> The guiding Hand,
> uplifting Hand,
> indicating Hand,
> revealing the path
> of Highest Law.

12

CREATIVITY AND HIERARCHY

Creative persons go from one phase of creativity to higher phases of creativity. Every act of creativity is associated with joy. Every simple, average, creative person expresses his emotions, his observations, his thoughts in an artistic way which becomes an attraction for many.[1]

This phase slowly fades away and he starts to create for the public. His inspiration comes from the suffering, pain, joy, and striving of the public. This kind of creativity has high power and lasts for a long time.

Eventually the creative person sees the vision, and his creativity is inspired by the Hierarchy and by the Plan. To this end, all his creativity was a preparation so that eventually he is able to hold his consciousness high enough to touch the inspiration of the Hierarchy and adequately formulate it in truth and in beauty.

Of course, this phase takes many lives, and the creative person matures in his efforts and totally becomes a transmitter of Hierarchical expressions. He has nothing to offer from

1. See *The Creative Fire*, Ch. 55.

himself. Actually his self has vanished. He has become a pure transmitter of Hierarchical expressions.

Great masterpieces will appear in coming decades by those who have consecrated their life for centuries to Hierarchical creativity. Their intelligence, love-wisdom, and power will be present in each creativity, and people will sense the beauty of their works.

Such kinds of creativity will create a high standard and, gradually, the works that were based on self-interest, vanity, ego, separation, and greed will vanish. Such kinds of art will lose their foundation, and artists will be forced to look for higher sources of inspiration.

The more the number of Hierarchically creative people increase, the more the world will transform.

To be successful in Hierarchical creativity, many old forms in the mental, emotional, and etheric planes must be destroyed. So we are expecting that creative destroyers will appear in the field of art and do their job.

This can be done in two ways: Artists who are highly critical will expose the futility of old art, outdated art based on the body, sex, personality, and even on individuality; or artists will come with such a potency of light and glory that average art will slowly vanish.

In the creative process, we see that creativity starts with the individual. Slowly the individual operates as a small group, then a larger group. When one reaches the level of Hierarchical creativity, the individual is assimilated into an advanced creative group, into an Ashram where everyone is engaged with the creative group work. This is why such group work is charged with high power and why they can move mountains. Many viewpoints, many angles, many talents are synthesized together to create and to express Hierarchical or Divine intention.

The Hierarchical creators will exercise their full speed to

create and relate with each other in order to strengthen the general expressions of the Hierarchical inspiration.

The Hierarchical creators have another step to attain, but at that time They will be Arhats Whose whole life will be a burning bush from the fire of the Will of God.

Such art and books can appear once in a century but, like a comet, leave behind their light for many centuries.

APPROACHING THE IDEA OF THE PLAN

Understanding of the Plan is a gradual process, an ever-expanding process, until the ocean of the Purpose is revealed. This process can be portrayed as entering into a palace.

First, for many years, man is as an ant traveling back and forth upon the outer stone walls. Then he is like a dog who guards the gate. Then as a human being, he is admitted to the outer court. Then as a neophyte, opportunity is given to him to see the kitchen. Then as a pledged disciple, he enters into the food storage room. Then as an accepting disciple, he is admitted to the antechamber of the Great Hall, where he stays for many incarnations. Then as an accepted disciple, he enters into the Great Hall.

As a first degree initiate, he sees the gate. As a second degree initiate, he is allowed to see the library. As a Third Degree Initiate, he is given a chance to see through the window the Crown and the Throne. As a Fourth Degree Initiate, he is allowed to see the Throne. As a Fifth Degree Initiate, he is allowed to see the Throne and the Crown. Here the full Plan of the Throne and Crown is revealed to his consciousness and all the duties and responsibilities of the Plan associated with them.

Who are the members of the Hierarchy? They are Higher Beings Who surpassed human evolution.

What is the Plan? The Plan is based on the process of perfection. "Be perfect as your Father in Heaven is perfect." The Plan is the procedure to make us attain that perfection.

13

TWELVE WAYS TO SERVE HIERARCHY

It is very important to participate in the service of Hierarchy through the following twelve ways:

- developing and practicing compassion and harmlessness
- dissipating fear
- emphasizing the immortality of the human soul
- creating right human relations
- abandoning greed and competition
- spreading the Teachings of the Ageless Wisdom
- speaking and writing about freedom and tolerance
- emphasizing one humanity
- dedicating our life to beauty and rejecting ugliness
- working for the purification of the planet
- dispersing superstition and prejudice
- living for reality

1. *Developing and practicing compassion and harmlessness.* Hierarchy stands for compassion and harmlessness. Trying to live a life of compassion and harmlessness helps Them to be successful in Their efforts to disperse hatred and separatism. Every effort to increase compassion and harmlessness in any department of human labor is a source of energy for Their efforts.

All these drops of compassion accumulate and turn into apparatuses in the hands of Hierarchy to bring to earth all healing influences of compassion.

2. *Dissipating fear.* Very soon groups will be formed to dissipate every form of fear because fear distorts reality and channels dark forces for destructive activities.

Every time a person dispels fear from another person, group, or nation, he does a great service for humanity. Such an activity cleans the communication lines between Hierarchy and humanity.

As long as fear remains in the psyche of people, they cannot receive the inspiration of Hierarchy nor can they follow Their instructions. To the degree that we get rid of fear, to that degree we cooperate with the efforts of Hierarchy.

We must know the nature of fear and attack it intelligently, with wisdom and courage. This is a service that pulls us closer to the heart of the Hierarchy.

3. *Emphasizing the immortality of the human soul.* The Hierarchy, through all Its great leaders throughout ages, has tried to illuminate the consciousness of the masses with the fact that human beings survive beyond the grave. But various agents throughout history only talked about death. They said that there is only matter, and that a man's existence ends with his death.

All disciples must mobilize and fight against this concept of death with the weapons of their experiences of immortality, with science, psychology, philosophy, and the Ageless Wisdom, and dispel this illusion of death. Those who try in any way to bring humanity the hope, the knowledge, and the joy of immortality are cooperating with the Hierarchy.

Disciples intuitively know that death does not exist. They must talk and write about this fact and produce great works of art promoting the immortality of the soul and its glorious destination. Special groups must be dedicated to carry out such work and to creatively enlighten humanity with fact, experiences, and wisdom, dispersing the dark existence of death from the consciousness of humanity.

4. *Creating right human relations*. This is a highly blessed service for the Hierarchy. In the Plan of the Hierarchy, this is a priority. There is a call for all humanity to develop and actualize right human relations in homes, in groups, in societies, in nations, in every way possible. Such a service will be a lifeboat for humanity to save it from final destruction.

Right human relations must be analyzed scientifically, philosophically, and psychologically from the viewpoints of business and science, from the viewpoint of international politics, from the viewpoints of harmony and cooperation, from the viewpoints of health and happiness. Groups must be formed to carry out such a job intelligently, sacrificially, and practically to help humanity see the value of right human relationships in every avenue of life.

5. *Abandoning greed and competition*. Hierarchy wants humanity to know that greed and competition robbed the natural resources on the planet, and that gradually we will face the consequences of greed and competition.

Greed and competition lead us to revolutions, to wars, to destruction.

In the future these facts will be clearly visible, and disciples in every field will illuminate people not to follow the destructive path of greed and competition.

Those in life who are trying to help people to see the dangers of greed and competition are servants of the Hierarchy. They are working under Their impression to help Hierarchy disperse such an evil, which prevents humanity from achieving great heights of health, happiness, and success.

Every time you are tempted by greed and competition, stop it! In that way you cooperate with the Hierarchy.

6. *Spreading the Teaching of the Ageless Wisdom.*[1] In all ages, the Hierarchy has sent Great Ones to teach humanity higher principles, higher laws, to set greater standards, to give vision and knowledge.

All the symphony of Their principles, laws, standards, visions, and knowledge are combined and called the Ageless Wisdom, which contains the highest virtues and the highest good for humanity.

Try to find this Teaching and spread it in the world. Help those who are dedicated to this task. Write books about these great universal principles and laws. Speak about them.

Put these principles into the arts. Make it available for groups and the masses. Read about the Ageless Wisdom and know about the Teaching so that you do not waste your money and time grazing in cheap pleasures. Help to distribute the Ageless Wisdom to illuminate the souls of men. Every time you help others to know and practice the Ageless Wisdom, you build the palace of the future for yourself and your loved ones.

The Ageless Wisdom is not religion but includes it. It is for everybody, like the air, like the water, like the sunshine. Distribute its light to your closest ones, to all those who are in the slavery of darkness.

This is a great service you can render to the Hierarchy. They will see your labor, and at the right time They will contact you for more daring labor.

7. *Speaking and writing about true freedom.* Hierarchy

---

1. See *The Ageless Wisdom.*

puts a tremendous effort into teaching humanity to be free. Slavery, in any form, is condemned by the Hierarchy. Those who work for freedom will be called the Knights of the Lord. Speak and write about freedom. Try to release people from physical, emotional, mental, even spiritual slavery. Your duty is to break prison bars from the human mind, heart, and life and to set the prisoners free.

Speak about the beauty of freedom. Tell people that there is no state of consciousness as glorious as the state of consciousness that is in the light of freedom.

In your daily life try to set people free. You can even exercise the art of freedom in your home, in your office, in any social contacts by acting intelligently in wisdom, in humility, and in courage. There are huge amounts of possibilities that one can do.

You can speak about freedom without using aggressive techniques, without imposition but through the wisdom of actualized freedom. Freedom and tolerance are the two pillars through which the Initiates pass to the Temple of Hierarchy.

Those who are free and those who are tolerant will see the Lord in their own innermost sanctuary and sit with Him at the Table of Wisdom.

8. *Emphasizing one humanity*. Hierarchy respects all nations and appreciates their customs and special characteristics but indicates that all nations are the stream from the One Source and are rising to the same Source. All nations must have their independence and freedom, but they must cooperate with each other for the Common Good. Eventually people will feel that the world is their home, and that we are all sisters and brothers.

One day the animosity among nations will disappear, and a deep cooperation will take place. Humanity will save so much energy, time, money, and life in building the real form of one humanity. People will be considerate of each other. The huge expansion of armies and police will be at a minimum. Business will bloom, and everyone will have some place to work. Travel will be unlimited, and everyone will benefit from the beauty of Nature. Humanity will be a big family.

9. Dedicating our life to beauty and rejecting ugliness. One of the efforts of the Hierarchy is to stimulate the sense of beauty in every division of life. Each beauty evokes higher cooperation, and energies released from such a cooperation enrich the life in all layers.

Every artist creating beauty will be blessed by the contact of Higher Forces: beauty in our manners, bodies, emotions, thoughts, visions, and goals; beauty in our homes, schools, offices, and environment; even beauty in courts and prisons will help raise the consciousness of humanity. That is the goal of the Hierarchy.

Slowly ugliness will not be able to find a place to hide and live. The transforming nation of human souls will reject ugliness as a suicidal disease and will become aware of contamination

Each ugliness brings discord to our aura, affects our health and happiness, and evokes ugly seeds planted within us.

Beauty creates mental, emotional, and physical health because it provides an atmosphere of harmony and upliftment.

We must start to trust the value of beauty in our children, in their ways of expression and make them tune in with the spark of beauty. The Hierarchy is the source of Beauty. Its teaching is Beauty. The constitution of the Teaching is the embodiment of Beauty.

10. Working for the purification of the planet. This is imperative. Most human beings understand the necessity to purify their systems. The planet also needs an intensive purification process.

The planet is full of toxins and waste, and the earth is polluted. This pollution is affecting our bodies, relationships, thinking, and creativity. A systemic purification is necessary. All those who are awakened to this issue must try to become the agent of purification in their environment.

Humanity will slowly degenerate. All living forms will slowly fade away if we continue to pollute our environment and live in it. All our culture and civilization, all our interests and labor will vanish if the foundation of purification is not solid and lasting.

We cannot expect higher culture and civilization while living in cesspools.

The Hierarchy has been making every effort to awaken humanity to the grave danger of pollution since 1900. Humanity was not sensitive enough to prevent the danger of pollution, which is mostly the result of greed, competition, and hatred.

Those who clean the environment and work internationally to purify the earth are the Children of Light who, with great sacrifice and nobility, want to save life on the planet.

11. *Dispersing superstition and prejudice*. Seventy percent of humanity live in superstition and prejudice, which means seventy percent of humanity have not expanded their consciousness and live in illusions and glamors. This creates a dark wall through which rays of enlightenment cannot penetrate into their being, and they live and act in darkness, affecting the life of humanity.

Prejudice and superstition are formations of ignorance, and they, by nature, cause separatism and toxicity. They contaminate facts and reality and change them into ugliness. As long as a person, a group, or a nation lives in superstition and prejudice, they prevent their consciousness from growing, expanding, and responding to the steps of evolutionary progress. Thus they become hindrances on the path of humanity and create friction with those forces which strive for the liberation of consciousness and freedom of spirit.

The Hierarchy is anxious to see people free from the

ragged, obsolete, and dirty clothes of superstition and prejudice and standing in the light of reality. Everyone who becomes
an agent to disperse prejudice and superstition serves not only
Hierarchy but also all humanity. Their names will shine in the
temples of Higher Worlds.

12. *Living for reality*. People lost the path leading to reality and often became their illusions, prejudices, superstitions,
day-dreaming, and glamors.

Art began to cover reality and lead people to unreality.
The duty of art is to reveal reality. The path of reality

- is to discover the laws and principles of Nature and to
  live a life accordingly
- leads to knowing oneself and living according to that
  knowledge
- is to choose the most essential in life and live for the
  most essential
- is the light which disperses all lies, pretensions, imita-
  tion, manipulation, exploitation and reveals those factors which lead to health, happiness, real success, and
illumination
- unveils the facts, the most essential, and the steps to
  take to actualize this in our life

The Hierarchy, for a long time, has been engaged in the
task of revealing beyond the unreal and helping humanity
walk on the path of reality. Those who fall from the path of
reality lose their sanity, health, and success, and they become
forced to serve the dark forces of ignorance, selfishness, and
separatism.

The ancient *Upanishad* said, "May we be led from the
unreal to the real."

This deep aspiration, hidden in the human heart, must
awaken. In fact, this aspiration exists in all kingdoms. It strives
to come to the surface of reality. Reality is the progressive

beingness which all existence realizes on the path of its unfoldment and progress. This is the path for every form of life to follow, the path of becoming the One Self.

The Hierarchy, ages ago, inspired humanity to be aware of illusions, glamors, deceit, and fabrications and to enter into the path of reality. Only the path of reality secures joy and glory to the advancing soul on the path of Infinity.

Every person, every group, every nation can serve Hierarchy. Their serving helps Them make life on the planet a glorious achievement with health, prosperity, success, and future bliss in the Higher Worlds.

THE EYES OF HIERARCHY

Urusvati is grateful to India and Tibet for their protection of the Brotherhood. One can be truly grateful that the concept of the Brotherhood is so carefully guarded. Usually, even talk about the Brotherhood is discouraged and names are not mentioned, for it is better even to deny the existence of the Brotherhood than to betray it. The legends about the Brotherhood are safeguarded, together with the sacred books.

The curiosity of the Western world is not understood in the East. Let us examine why the West wants to know about the Brotherhood. Does the West wish to emulate the Brotherhood in daily life? Does the West wish to preserve the Ordainments of the Brotherhood? Does the West wish to deepen its knowledge? So far they show only idle curiosity and look for reason to criticize and blame. We shall not help them on this path.

Let us imagine a military expedition that discovers the Brotherhood. One can easily imagine the outcome of such a discovery, and the curses and anathemas that would follow! Crucifixions take place even today. Thus the West has never understood the essence of Our Hierarchy. The concept of dictatorship does not fit Our Hierarchy. We have established as law the idea that power lies in sacrifice. Who among today's leaders will accept this Ordainment?

We well understand the nature of the East, and because of its nature one should all the more note its reverence for Our Abode. Many Ashrams were transferred to the Himalayas because the atmosphere of the other locations had become intolerable. The last Egyptian Ashram was transferred to the Himalayas because of the well-known events in Egypt and the adjoining regions. At the beginning of Armageddon all the Ashrams had to be gathered together in the Abode in the Himalayas. It should be known that at present We do not leave Our Abode, and We go to distant places only in Our subtle bodies. Thus the records about the inner life of Our Abode are being revealed.

Supermundane I, para. 19
Agni Yoga Society

When I was a small boy one of my Teachers explained to me that "Great joy is experienced in heaven in the hearts of the Great Ones when people gather together in the name of Beauty, Goodness, Righteousness, Joy, Freedom, service, and striving, in the name of the Hierarchy, in the name of Christ." This is because when people gather in the name of the Hierarchy or in the name of Christ, they create a whirlpool of energy, and that whirlpool of energy attracts the wisdom of the Hierarchy, Their energy, Their beauty, Their impressions and inspirations. Eventually, charged with these energies, we use them for our health, happiness, for our spiritual progress, even in our businesses and in our relationships. Eventually we become small, small springs of fresh water for humanity. That is how nations and humanity are transformed.

Nations and humanity are transformed only by those people who build a link between earth and those who have achieved great success in their spiritual advancement. In the future you will realize that those nations that are prosperous, that are becoming the leaders of humanity, all have disciples and Initiates Who linked themselves with the Sources of Light, Life, Love, and Beauty.

That is what we are doing in a sense. We are in this nation. We are serving this nation by bringing new inspirations, new impressions, new energies. Throughout our relationships we are spreading these energies to our nation, to many levels of our nation, and to many levels of humanity. If the number of people who have dedicated their life to Light, Love, Beauty, Goodness, Righteousness, and striving increase, or if the numbers of these people who have connections with higher sources increases, that nation will be powerful and will lead the world into economic and spiritual heights.

Each of us can be counted through our striving, through our focus on Hierarchy. In talking about Hierarchy and thinking about Hierarchy, we charge ourselves. After charging ourselves, we will see how it will affect our health, happiness, joy, family relationships, group relationships, and our relationships with our nation and humanity as a whole. Once every month, once every week, once every day, even once every hour, your thoughts must go to the Hierarchy. The Great Sage says that, "Eventually those people who are advancing in humanity will think, will feel, will act in the Presence of Hierarchy." If your consciousness shifts and brings you to the Presence of the Hierarchy, you will see that you are an inspired, inflamed, fiery, dedicated human being who is spreading a new transforming light everywhere and in everything. That is your glory. Your glory, your progress depend on how much you contribute to human transformation.

We think, for example, that this planetary life does not

have a captain, any blueprint, any plan. Everybody comes and goes and does anything he wants. It is chaos. But the reality is that all of you, from birth to death, are watched by the Eyes of Hierarchy. That is sometimes very scary. If suddenly you realize that big "eyes" are watching you and your every move is recorded in the archives of the Hierarchy, it sometimes scares you. And sometimes you feel that your best deeds, best wishes, best feelings, best thoughts are not lost. They are accumulated in the archives of the Hierarchy.

The world for the Hierarchy is an organized computer. In the computer, each of our names is there. When you become a first degree initiate, your name starts flashing in the computer, and They put your name into another computer where advanced people, advancing Initiates watch your name and what is happening to you. Sometimes for three years, for three lives, for thirty lives, They watch you to see what difference you are making in your life, how you are progressing, how you are failing, how you are coming into defeat, victory, or success or how sometimes, in a heroic act, you sacrifice yourself to bring transformation into the life of your nation.

The idea that is going to remain in your mind is this: In the computer of the Hierarchy, not a single action, feeling, or word of yours is lost. It is all recorded there. According to your records you will be promoted in the ranks of the Hierarchy, until one day you will be ready to consciously communicate with Them. Before you are ready, your name is not in the computer because your presence creates upheaval and destruction in the computer of the Hierarchy, and because you are too violent to be in that subtle computer.

One of the great Masters says that there is a great, huge underground cave, and all the walls of the cave are decorated with little, little images. They are the images of those people who took the first initiation. A crew of Initiates watches the images everyday and sees how your image is changing. It is just like the images of x-rays. There is a little spark there. There is a little spark going, a new life is coming, life is disappearing. Each day the Great Ones watch you, especially if you are an advanced Initiate.

Day after day They watch, and if They see that your color is changing, your note is changing, your name on the computer has a red color. That red has seventy-seven degrees of redness, hues. Each hue signifies something. Colors are the alphabet with which to read the x-ray records.

Each color is associated with a note. They hear the note and They say, "The physical note of this man has static. He is sick. The physical note of this man or woman is very clear, and it has a chord in it, harmony in it, symphony in it." So that man physically, emotionally, mentally is growing and becoming radioactive. When They see that your composition is changing and that your life is gradually transforming, They send a Ray to your image. Immediately you feel it without knowing what is happening to you. But afterward you say, "You know, tomorrow I am going to get up early in the morning and say my prayers, do my meditation. For a long time I have not done my lessons. Let me start them. This book I started, but I never finished it. Let me finish it. Let me go and visit my friend who is in the hospital. I have forgotten about him. Let me help these people. Let me give one million dollars to this hospital, to this temple, to this university." Something happens to you, but it is not the result of your logic. It is the result of a contact that They made with you because They think you are valuable and have merit enough to have a contact with Their energy of inspiration. Nothing is given in the Universe without being worthy of it. That is a great law. You must be worthy of it because, if you are not worthy of it you misuse this energy, this inspiration, this vision. You are going to use the energy you receive in your business, in your life, in whatever level. The energy is a gift for you because you became worthy of it.

Then They test you to see how this grace, these blessings given to you are used in your life. They see if you are using the energy to cheat people, to harm people, to destroy and manipulate people, or if you are using the energy to transform the world.

What is Their supreme goal for humanity? There is only one thing: It is to reveal the Divinity that is hidden within us, to make us Divine beings.

You remember Christ said, "You are going to do greater things than I did if you follow My steps." We did not do that yet. Imagine what a great individuality He was. We did not do it yet because the powers or the great potentials we have within us have not yet been released. The Hierarchy helps us release these potentials within us and gradually, gradually makes us walk and proceed on the path of perfection.

Yesterday you were a chemical compound. Then you became a vegetable. Then you became a tree, a flower, and so on. Then you became an animal, and the animal became human. The human kingdom is one of the kingdoms that we are going to surpass. It has now been twenty million years, and most of humanity have not changed their kingdom. Now we are going to enter the fifth, sixth, seventh kingdoms.

If our spiritual evolution had proceeded according to the Plan, most of us would have etheric, astral, and mental control by the year 2000. Because of this control, we would have a very refined and healthy life. But most of us are left behind. There are those who are advanced enough to control their astral and mental bodies and thus proceed to higher kingdoms. All this can be done through striving and by getting closer to the Hierarchy.

What is the prime target of the Hierarchy? It is to release the Divinity that is living within us. It is to make us able to have a fuller and greater life, not being stuck to our bodies, not being stuck to our homes, refrigerators, and heaters, but to surpass them like angels, like great Initiates. We do not need the telephone, telegram, radio, and television because they are all in our being, but they have not been released yet. We do not even need airplanes because we can travel spiritually.

The other day a Master from the Himalayas came to a friend's house, said a few words, then went back. He said, "I called you three times, and you did not hear My voice." He traveled seven thousand miles. In one second, He went to the man's house and returned to the Himalayas. That is what we are going to become.

I was in Jordan once. A holy man visited my office. He gave me some incense, talked a few minutes, and left. I went out to see him, but he was not there. That night when another friend and I were sitting in my home, a message came for us from that holy man saying that he was now in Mecca and would soon be back in a few days. People knew that he could travel in his body wherever he wanted to go.

Your brain is a computer. Each computer is hooked with every other computer and with the great Computer of the Hierarchy. Hierarchy knows immediately what you are thinking, what your plan and purpose is. They are aware of it because They live in an omnipresent condition within our mind and within the minds of all people.

We are going to develop the sense, the consciousness that we are always watched and that we are living in the presence, in the consciousness of the Hierarchy. Because we are living in the presence, in the consciousness of the Hierarchy, we are going to learn day after day how to be the best that we can be. That means that all our life is going to be a life of striving toward perfection. How are you dressing? How are you communicating with each other? How is your heart? How is your emotional body? How are your feelings? How is your thinking? What is your plan? What are you doing to help humanity, to transform humanity? What kind of future goals do you have in your mind? According to all these different thoughts, feelings, and activities, you put the records of the image you have in the caves of the Himalayas. These records decide your future incarnations, your future pain and suffering, your future success, blessings, and achievements.

I was reading a book called *Supermundane*. In that book the Great Sage says, "If only once you hear the singing of the Brothers in the Hierarchy, you will not be the same person." Then He adds, "Hierarchy means heavy labor to Infinity without any imposition. By Our free will We are dedicated to the transformation of humanity. We do these things with the utmost joy." It is a great sign when every good servant, every advancing man starts doing his job, his duty, his responsibility with great joy because responsibility is given to you to serve humanity, in the best way that you can, to bring health, happiness, success, prosperity, and freedom to humanity.

THE HISTORY OF HIERARCHY

Our earth has seven bodies. Just as our earth has, you also have seven bodies. You have the physical-etheric body, and this is the physical body. Then you have the astral, mental, Intuitional, Atmic, Monadic, and Divine bodies. In some schools they call these seven principles. These seven bodies are the bodies through which you function on corresponding planes of the planet.

We are living now in the physical body. For example, your physical body goes through seven phases of evolution. Your emotional body goes through seven phases of evolution as does your mental body. This happens without your being conscious of it, but if you are consciously developing these bodies, you go faster and faster. As you go faster, you become happier, healthier, more prosperous and successful. But if you delay your evolution, you develop more pain and suffering, failure and defeat.

The purpose of the Teaching of the Hierarchy is to make us able to use all seven bodies, just as we use our physical body. Perfection is the ability to use all these bodies and through them have a greater field of communication, experience, and information with the Existence as a whole.

Before us, there were four Root Races. The First Race was a very etheric race. The Second Race was a little denser. The Third Race was called the Lemurian Race. They were controlled by Divine leaders and needed individual development.

Each of you has a Guardian Angel, Who is an extension of the computer of the Hierarchy in you, and Who reports what is going on within your system every minute. Even in the *Bible* Christ said, "Your Angel is there and every day contacts the Father in Heaven." What was He talking about? "Father in Heaven" is a very symbolic phrase. It means that there is some Center around the earth which collects the needed information of those who are on the path. Your Angel, every day, sees the face of your Father and communicates with Him. In modern language, it means the computer is immediately transferring the data of your life, physically, emotionally, and mentally to the data system that is in the Hierarchy.

Now how is Hierarchy built? These 105 Great Beings built the educational system on the planet to teach humanity seven fields of knowledge. They started with the ABCs. The first thing that was taught was politics, very basic politics, for example, how to relate with each other, how to lead people, how to organize people, how to use the power of the people through cooperation. This was the political department of the Hierarchy, which was in the hands of a great Master. Everywhere in the world They started to teach classes on leadership through their disciples and Initiates.

The second department was education. They started to

collect those people who were a little smarter, a little more awakened, who were striving a little more. They started to teach education. Education was the science of self-revelation, self-knowledge.

The third department established by the Hierarchy was communication, how to communicate with each other. If you read history, the myths and mythologies of humanity, you will see that the communication system was a masterpiece system, how They invented the hieroglyphics and drums to communicate through motions and symbols, how to start speaking and building different words to express themselves through voice, and so on. It is all a communication system. They started to teach communication to all humanity.

The fourth department established was the arts. If you are a student of the arts, you will see that in very, very early times humanity was occupied by very primitive art, but it was art. Art was the only method to make you creative, bringing your ideas and thoughts into manifestation. For example, you visualize a beautiful flower. That is inside of you. When you bring that flower into the pencil and draw it, you feel that a part of yourself is coming out of you. This is the initial step to externalize the powers and potentials which are latent within man.

The fifth department was the establishment of the scientific field. They started to teach primitive science. Eventually they taught about the wheel, axles, metals, and different things. Eventually science advanced and advanced and came to this age with the science that we have now. It was all started by the Hierarchy.

The development of science in the Hierarchy is the source which inspires our scientists. It projects into their mind those formations which will help the progress of humanity. Most of our scientific discoveries are distorted reflections of what Hierarchy tries to impress upon the minds of scientists.

For example, let us take television. Two Great Sages say

that "We have mirrors in our groups which we can turn toward any person and watch what he or she is doing." For example, a disciple was walking and the Master was watching him. Suddenly, He saw that a big tower was going to fall on the disciple's head. He immediately shouted, "Stop there," and the disciple was saved. They do not call it television. They call it "the mirrors." This can be important for you to know. It will be a warning system in your mind to know that you are on television. It is a big Eye that is watching you, but They never criticize you. They never hate you. They just want you to know what you are. They want to help you so that your evolution proceeds and you transform your nature and eventually become worthy of working in an Ashram in the Hierarchy.

The sixth department was religion. They started to give the religious ideals, very primitive religious ideas. The first idea they gave to humanity at that time was that there is a connection between man and the Creator. You can find this in the oldest religions, oldest traditions, and in myths and legends. Religion means direct communication with the Almighty One. Our present religions are television religions. If I ask, "Are you a religious person," and you say, "Yes," it means that you would be able to communicate daily with God consciously. Are you in communication? Look how backward we are saying we are religious people. Intellectually we are assuming that there is a Great Being, and one of His Sparks is within us and that we can communicate with Him. But we do not know how to communicate with Him consciously. Those who were able to communicate with Higher Intelligent forces unfolded their potentials, and, life after life, dedicated themselves to teaching humanity how to communicate with the Central Light in their system and on earth.

I remember Ohannes Chelebian, who was my Teacher. He was an Armenian, and he was very universal. Day and night he was in meditation. One day I went to his home. I said,

119

"It is twelve thirty. Have you eaten anything?" He said, "I have not eaten. Can you go and bring some bread and some olives for me?" I hesitated because I did not have a penny and did not know how I was going to pay for the bread and olives. He knocked a box on the table and seventy-five cents came out. This was a great shock for me, though I never showed him that I was shocked. I looked at the money, put it in my pocket, and brought him what he wanted. I was always looking at the box thinking about what he did. To test him I said, "Master, don't you need a little onion?" He said, "Yes, I think onion is good." He knocked again, and the money appeared. I went immediately to a friend. I said, "Give me twenty-five, cents and you take this twenty-five cents. Keep it." I wanted to spend my friend's twenty-five cents. Later, I wanted my friend to return it because it was very precious to me, but he never gave it back because I told him it was something miraculous. He said, "If it is miraculous, I will not give it back." I brought the onion back to my Teacher and he asked, "How did you bring this onion?" I answered, "With money." "Which money?" he asked and smiled. He knew I kept his twenty-five cents. Then he said, "Open your palm." He put four twenty-five cent pieces in my palm. I asked, "What is this?" He answered, "Ask and it will be given." I kept that money for ten, fifteen years until it was later stolen. This is an example of communication with Higher Forces.

Christ never lied when He said, "Ask and it will be given. Knock and the door will be opened." We have experienced this. Whenever we made a book ready for publication, the money has come surprisingly. We believe that the Invisible Forces help us to serve Them.

The seventh department Hierarchy established was business. They taught how to do business in its various branches. The seventh department also taught the science of ceremonies and divine magic.

These teachings went out for about one million years. After one million years, the Great Ones came to humanity to walk among men. They were the first Ones Who became kings and queens and the heads of all departments of human endeavor. They taught the most sophisticated sciences to humanity, the Fourth Race. This science was so advanced that the Great Sage says, "Our technology now is less advanced than at that time," because all technology was in the hands of these 105 Kumaras, the Great Ones. If their land comes out of the ocean, we will find paradises, airplanes, radios, and televisions and other things which were the most sophisticated things for that time.

They formed the Hierarchy, and the Hierarchy became a great institution. We are told that They formed in Central America, in the Gobi Desert, in India, in Caucasia, in Mount Ararat, in Russia, in the North Pole. There were seven big universities. The Aztec and Mayan civilizations were the result of universities which They built there. When They formed these universities, They slowly, slowly took disciples. The disciples advanced and became initiated in seven degrees. If one from humanity was initiated to the Third Degree, one of the Masters left the Hierarchy and went to His star. We are told that now all the Hierarchy is from humanity, and the beauty is that Hierarchy is formed from all nations. There is no one nation there. It is Chinese, it is Arabic, it is Jewish, it is Armenian, it is German, it is French. All of Hierarchy is built by all nations, and They are so coordinated that the Great Sage says, "We are like one nervous system." Everything is coordinated everywhere.

Masters utilize the energy of the Rays and their cycles to bring various changes in human life and consciousness. Every Ray appearing or disappearing gives Them an opportunity to utilize situations to help humanity. Changes in Nature provide great help to them to use the cycles and bring new adjustment

121

to the life of the planet.

They are like the helmsman of a boat which is going through the rapids; each change in the current evokes a new way of directing the boat. Changes in energy currents provide new opportunities to bring in constructive results. When the situation in the world deteriorates due to new and increasing energies, They take such a condition as an opportunity to use new energies for regeneration.

Their method is to broadcast ideas and visions or to transmit a certain Teaching to Their disciples to spread in the world in order to create responses toward new energies.

Our solar system is not the Heart Center of that "One" but the heart center of a constellation which acts as the Heart Center of the One, which is one of the seven systems around the "One."

The great mysteries of Initiations were given to our humanity by the Hierarchy, Who, we are told, records them from the White Lodge of Sirius.

Question: Which planet did They come from?

Answer: That is a very technical question. They came from one of the schemes of Venus. It is a little difficult. They came from a distant planet where the civilization is so advanced that the most advanced human beings on this planet are equal to ants in Their Presence. That is what the Great Teacher says. For example, the most advanced scientist on earth is an ant compared to a scientist who is living there.

Our Hierarchy is the reflection of the Headquarters of a greater Hierarchy, which is in the star Sirius. Sirius is a Cosmic center and the real headquarters of our planetary Hierarchy. Of course, there are other Galactic centers controlling other higher Hierarchies.

Question: How can we become a member of the Hierarchy?

Answer: Hierarchy established two kinds of schools: exoteric schools and esoteric schools. Exoteric schools are like our schools, colleges, and universities in which we learn our material science, physical science, objective science. That is very important for us. In esoteric schools They teach, for example, how to leave your body and stay out of your body; how to live in space without a body, without even an emotional body; how to use your mental body and work in the mental planes, and so on. They teach how to travel from one planet to another planet; how to hear mentally the thoughts and feelings of other people; how to inspire people and direct their lives toward perfection and striving and beauty by challenging and inspiring people.

To do these things They organized a school which is called the School of Initiation. All secret societies and most of the religions are distortions of these schools.

THE SCHOOL OF INITIATION

The School of Initiation is divided into seven layers. You take the first initiation when you become the master of your body. No longer does your body control you. You control your body and, one day in your dream or in your awakened consciousness, They take you into the school and test you to see if you can control your body and leave your body. To do this They have four tests. The four tests are the test of fire, the test of air, the test of earth, and the test of water.

Sometimes some of you passed these tests in your dreams. For example, you stand on a big mountain and someone pushes you to the abyss, and you suddenly awaken. You did not pass because you were thinking you were in the body. You were still identified with your body. If you are identified with your body, you cannot detach yourself from your body. For example, suddenly you are in the fire. You panic and you awaken. But if you are without a body, you like the fire, and the fire does not burn you. You must pass these kinds of tests.

The first initiation is that you really control your physical urges and drives. No longer does your body control you, your sex control you, your appetite control you, or drugs, dope, and cigarettes control you. You do not have any habits anymore. You can control them.

Then when They see that for one life, two lives, you are really controlling your physical body, you go to the first classroom. In this classroom They teach how to ooze out from your body every night. It is very scientific. I have contacted and talked with many people who passed through these exercises and initiations. It is a fantastic thing. You can sleep and immediately go anywhere you want with your etheric or astral or mental body. This is done in the first initiation.

The second initiation is the purification of your astral body. The astral body is your emotions. There are six things which you must conquer. They are fear, anger, hatred, jealousy, revenge, and malice. If you control these six vipers you slowly, slowly become ready to enter into the second degree of initiation. It is very, very difficult because every day you are tested. You are tested by telephone calls, by your friends, by your wife and husband. Suddenly you become so angry, so vicious, and you shout and curse. Then you become jealous and revengeful. You did not pass the test.

Every life you can get a little closer to the Hierarchy. These six vices, six vipers are so sticky, like blacktop. Once they stick to you, it is hard to get rid of them. If you want to advance toward the Hierarchy and eventually enter into the door of the Hierarchy, you are going to control, especially, these six vipers.

Hatred must be totally uprooted from your system, hatred toward anybody, toward any nation, toward any religion. Hatred must be stopped because hatred prevents you from contact with Hierarchy.

Fear means you are identified with transient values, with your body, with things that are not continuously valuable, with your chair, with your jewels, with your furniture, with your business, with your body, with your friend's body, with your friend's possessions. You are identified. When these identifications are broken, you do not have any fear. Fear comes from identification. Fear and anger force you to impose your will upon others. If anyone does not do what you want them to do, you get angry. If you look at anger in your emotional plane, it is like a cancer. In the future, in three, four, five, ten lives, if you continue, anger turns into tumors, then cancer. You are going to overcome it by all means.

In the monasteries they told us they were going to take a few people to the mountains and leave them there. We were left in the mountains without any protection. Three or four days later, when we returned they would ask us, "Were you afraid?" "Of course, yes." But, a few people were never afraid. They said, "Let anything that will happen, happen." There was no fear.

You have millions of fears: body fear, emotion fear, money fear, business fear, divorce fear, marriage fear, children fear. Try to fight against them. If you have fear or any one of these six vipers, it means that you are going to labor to overcome it, if you want to enter into the second class of initiation.

Someone may ask, "If I do not want to progress, what happens? I do not want to enter into the first class. I do not want to enter into the second class. What happens then?" What happens is that you continue incarnating on this planet, year after year, life after life, continuously, and the planet becomes more polluted, more devastated, more criminal, and more uninhabitable, so you have doomed yourself. Eventually you turn into an animal, characteristically, and you want to finish your life on this planet and disappear. They take you to a lower planet where the life is animal-like. The more you retrogress, the more pain you invite into your life.

When you finish the second initiation, the Third Initiation opens, and the Great Ones start teaching mentally in your dreams. Maybe some of you attend classes at night. Have you had that experience? Have you attended classes where someone spoke, and then you remembered everything. You can even write in your diary that this and this wisdom was given to you in your dream. That is the mental plane.

How does it happen? You have five vipers in the mental plane which resist and prevent you from entering into the mental hall. It is a very advanced university, the mental plane. What are these guardians, these dogs that prevent you from entering there? One is called separatism — it is one of the greatest poisons in the human mind. It devastates humanity. Second is fanaticism. Third is vanity. Vanity means three things. A man says, "I know," but he does not know. That is vanity. A man says, "I can do everything," but he cannot do anything. He is vain. He says, "I have everything," but he does not have anything. It is vanity. That vanity creates some diseases in the mental plane. That disease prevents him from being able to live in the pressure of the mental plane university. These words are very interesting — "the pressure." You cannot stand the pressure of the mental plane, the fiery pressure, if you have vanity.

The fourth one is ego. "I am better than everybody. Everybody must serve me. I am great." You think that you are somebody, and you are not. That is ego. You want everybody to serve you, to respect you, to do anything possible for you to fit your ego. You are going to control that ego with humility, saying, "I am one of the servants of humanity. I will do my best so that everybody else around me can do their best, and I am one with them." Humility is cooperation with everything that exists.

The fifth one is greed. As you can see, humanity is devastating itself with the sickness of greed from those groups, those nations, those institutions who are pumping into the minds of humanity everyday, "Money, money, greed, greed, have, have, more, more, that is not enough, have more." These are great obstacles to initiation.

The Hierarchy used to teach all this ten, fifteen million years ago in secret brotherhoods and tested people on how they were acting, how they were passing through these tests. When they were tested, they would go through the experience of Transfiguration. This is very beautiful. In all religions these experiences are spoken of. Great disciples pass through this Initiation. Transfiguration is an experience in which you see that every cell of your body radiates the light that it has. It is a light violet color. A clairvoyant sees the violet. All the body becomes violet. Then the emotional body becomes all silvery. Then the mental body becomes all golden and yellow mixed together. Then you see a radiant Chalice in these three bodies transforming. Transfiguration is the unification of the fires or light in your three bodies, physically, emotionally, mentally.

Ten, fifteen million years ago, when you were transformed and passed the Transfiguration ceremony, you became the head of an Ashram. The Masters called you an Initiate and said, "Now you have five hundred people in your study group. You guide them, you lead them, you transform them, you challenge them, you exercise them, you discipline them. They are in your hands."

We are told that Krishna was the first One Who attained the Hierarchical leadership when He finished the Third Initiation. Christ became the Head of the Hierarchy when He finished the Fifth Initiation. The other one who is going to be the Head of the Hierarchy must finish the Seventh Initiation. Every ten thousand million years, They are advancing. For example, we had doctors five hundred years ago. They used to study three, four years and then they became doctors. Now you need to study maybe ten years, then many branches of healing.

Actually, you need ten or fifteen years to become a doctor. It is the same with initiations.

When you finish the Third Initiation, you achieve the Fourth Initiation of the Hierarchy. This Fourth Initiation is a very drastic initiation because the Fourth Initiation is called, in esoteric schools, separation of the spirit from the form. In Christian terminology, it is called crucifixion. In the Buddhist religion, it is called renunciation, total renunciation. For example, when Buddha went home at night and looked at His wife sleeping, looked at His baby sleeping, He said, "I am leaving. Good-bye to everybody." That was renunciation. He renounced His kingdom, His throne, jewels, riches, and glory. He renounced it all, and He proved that He had renounced. He became a Fourth Degree Initiate. Jesus became a Fourth Degree Initiate when they crucified Him.[1]

The inner meaning is not the crucifixion, which you are seeing outside. The inner meaning is the separation of the spirit from the bodies. In the Fourth Initiation you really are trained, maybe two, three, four lives, maybe sixty years, seven hundred years, seven thousand years to learn how to enter into your physical body and go out of it, enter into your emotional body and go out, enter into your mental body and go out, and to totally cut the control of the bodies upon you so that you are total spirit. In this process, from the Third Degree on, your physical body, emotional body, and mental body slowly lose all sicknesses, all disorders, all disharmony. They slowly, slowly melt away and you become a candidate for "Mastership."

The Fourth Initiation is the total dedication of yourself. Whatever you are, whatever you have, whatever you know is going to be sacrificed for the evolution, for the perfection of humanity. It is humanity, not your race, not your religion, not your group, that is important. It is the entire humanity. That is

---

1. See *Buddha Sutra: A Dialogue with the Glorious One.*

the Fourth Initiation. Of course, there are many, many tests. We are told that sometimes it is a three-year test, a thirty-year test, a three-hundred year test, a three-thousand year test until you reach the condition of a diamond. You become a diamond. The charcoal slowly, slowly, throughout the ages, becomes a diamond. This is the life. Life has a meaning, life has a plan, and every one of you is in the computer. Do not forget that. You are in the computer. How long do you want to stay on the lower level? That is up to you. When do you want to graduate and become a masterpiece, a Master, so that you start working in the Hierarchy?

Once you enter into the Fourth Initiation you do not use reason and logic anymore. You know everything exactly at that moment. You look at something and know the totality of it. That is the Intuitional Plane.

When you enter into the Atmic level you become a Master, and your consciousness works there. A Master is one Who totally became a bridge between humanity and the highest captain of the planet. He became a bridge. There are no cleavages between Him and God, so to speak. He became the bridge. That is why in the Ageless Wisdom every Master was called a bridge. Every Fourth Degree Initiate is called a bridge-builder. A Third Degree Initiate is called the laborer, collecting the stones of the bridge. The second degree initiate is one who is watching the blueprint of the bridge. The first degree initiate is told the fairy tales of being the bridge. These are very ancient and symbolic explanations of the paths of initiation.

When you became a bridge, it means you became a bridge between your physical, emotional, and mental bodies and the Divinity within you. There is no separation. You are a circuit now. You are one. There is no physical, emotional, and mental body. You are not only one with everything that exists but also one with humanity; you are one with the planet; you are one with the Soul of the planet; you are one with the Creator of the planet. You became one. That is the Atmic level. The highest power of the Atmic level is not intuition. It is called actualization, which means whatever you want now, at this moment, is done. For example, Christ said, "Stop," and all the waves stopped. He went to the dead man and said, "Get up!" There is no knowingness. There is no reason and logic anymore. It is instantaneous actualization.

Sixth Degree Initiates go to the Monadic level. The Sixth Degree Initiate is one Who can decide to stay on this planet or go to another planet. For example, our Hierarchy is formed by those Masters Who decided to stay with humanity until the majority of humanity enters into the Third Initiation. After the Third Initiation, They will leave.

With the Seventh Initiation, the Master finishes this earth evolution and acts in the Cosmic Astral Plane. We have a few Seventh Degree Initiates. Already they are acting in the Cosmic Astral Plane. We have the Cosmic Physical Plane, Cosmic Astral Plane, and higher Cosmic Planes. A Seventh Degree Initiate is a baby born in the Cosmic Astral Plane. Look how much we need to grow and expand and how deplorable it is that we waste our time doing things that are not contributing to our eternal progress and actualization. This is a very important thing: How much waste of time, how much waste of energy, how much waste of money is going toward things which are not related to our eternal progress and achievement? This is something you are going to think about. All our efforts must be directed toward perfection. Christ gave the highest advice. "Be perfect as your Father in heaven is perfect." What a great message it was, that the only goal in life is not to make money, to have high positions, possessions, to shine with glory, but only to reach perfection.

Perfection is threefold. The Third Degree Initiate is a perfect man. The Fifth Degree Initiate is a perfect Soul. The

Seventh Degree Initiate is a perfect Spirit. It has three layers — perfect, perfect, perfect, which is a very complicated thing.

Question: What was the Lemurian Race that you were speaking about? If some were so perfect, then why did Atlantis happen?

Answer: Lemurian people were not perfect. Masters were guiding them, teaching them so that they would start a movement toward perfection. When Masters withdraw, the races start to degenerate more and more. In Atlantis they had the highest civilization. The Great Teacher and the Great Sage say that they had airplanes which used to go faster than the speed of light. It was unimaginable perfection, but the Atlantean race degenerated because some people, who came from another solar system to evolve here, started to create the evil lodge. Then white magicians and black magicians fought there. It was so bad that Atlantis sank and disappeared.

Question: Will you say a little bit about what happens to the Solar Angel at the Fourth Initiation?

Answer: At the Fourth Initiation our Solar Angel, our Guardian Angel, leaves us, not because we are bad, but because we have reached the Fourth Initiation and do not need It. Until the Fourth Initiation, They follow you. Even in the Fourth Initiation, They do not live within you. They are around you. They come and make suggestions. You can even speak with It. For example, Goethe says that one day he was having lunch, and his Solar Angel sat in front of him. He had the most exceptional dialogue with his Angel. This is in his books. He was a very advanced man, a spiritual man. If you read *Faust*, it is a very nice book as a history, as a drama, but behind *Faust* is all esoteric teaching, which you are going to read from a different level.

Question: How does karma form a cloud?

Answer: A cloud is formed by your wrong actions, negative emotions, or polluted thinking. Every time your bodies are forced to do something against the Law of Nature and against the law of your conscience, they emanate a gas, an element, which accumulates in the body which took the wrong actions. Their accumulations are the seeds of future sicknesses.

There is also karma which is created through non-action. That is the other part of it. For example, you were supposed to do something, and you did not do it. That is a form of karma. You were supposed to say something now, and you did not because of your fear, because of your hesitation. It formed karma because you did not do it. You planned something beautiful, and you did not do it when you could do it. That is also karma. For example, say that a man is dying, and you are just passing by. You could have made a sandwich and fed the man. You did not do it. Your heart told you to do it. You did not do it. It is bad karma in your aura. Not only what you do makes karma or non-karma but also *what you do not do*, *what you do not think*, *what you do not say* create a karma.

All my books are written on this Teaching. There is nothing in my books that is outside of the Teaching. Read them. I have written for your level so that you understand them. For example, read the *Buddha Sutra* very carefully. It is a masterpiece. I read it fifteen times before publishing it. The other day I said, "Let me see what kind of book this is." I was on page eighty and I cried three times. It is fantastic. It is so beautiful. Read other books. *Cosmic Shocks* is very important. Read *The Psyche and Psychism* and *Challenge for Discipleship*. Read them very carefully, and make it a regular study, every day, because you are going to slowly think more and more about Hierarchy. In your daily works, think about Hierarchy, that They are watching you. One glorious day They are going to meet you and invite you for greater service.

I was a small boy, and I did not know very good English

yet. I opened the *Personal Memoirs of H.P. Blavatsky* and read it. I became very hot. I was inspired. I was energized, but I thought, "I do not understand what she is saying." I brought a monk, and he translated that section for me. In that section Blavatsky says, "One night when I was in London, it was a full moon, and I was on the bridge. A tall man looked at me and started to walk toward me. When I saw Him, I realized I used to see Him in my dreams. He came and hugged me and told me this, this, this. *It was the most memorable day of my life.*" I said, "Repeat it again." When the monk started reading the passage again, I cried. I felt that I was Blavatsky, and the Master was seeing me and teaching me. This is the glory of the human being.

15

THE PURPOSE AND THE PLAN

Hierarchy is composed of all those human beings who graduated from the level of human beings and have entered into superhuman evolution. All of you, in the right time, will graduate from this misery that we are in. You will graduate from your pains and sorrows, from your deaths and sufferings, from your loves and hates and jealousies. Eventually you will see that these are nothing, and you will dedicate yourself for the purpose of evolution, for the purpose of life.

We are playing a game in our life, and we do not know that we are losing time and energy doing things which we are not supposed to do and running after things that we should not run after. Thus, we are forgetting our prime purpose.

People do not know about the Hierarchy, and they do not think about the Hierarchy. But thinking and talking about the Hierarchy and reading about the Hierarchy make the Hierarchy real in our life. We establish a communication line between Hierarchy and ourselves. This is very important.

The Great Sage says that the Hierarchy has an apparatus, a machine, that registers every time people talk about Them.

When you say "Hierarchy" and talk about It, that machine registers it. It is so important to connect with Hierarchy so that the energies of the Hierarchy, the light and the love and the direction that are coming from the Hierarchy guide your life. Without Hierarchy, we are lost in the vast desert of creation. We do not have any goal; we do not have any direction; we do not know where we are going. And, after we die, we are lost in the sandstorm.

Hierarchy is now built and composed all from human beings. First, it was composed of Kumaras, great, advanced human beings who finished their course in previous solar systems. They graduated from their human evolution millions of years ago. They came to our planet and established the Hierarchy. Slowly, slowly, They left the Hierarchy and human beings took Their place. This is very important to know. Average man, the average American, never thinks about this. They are very busy with their jobs, with their pains and sufferings, with their hospitals, teeth, ears, eyes, and so on, but the main thing is to think about the Hierarchy.

It took eighteen million years for human beings to graduate, to be initiated, and eventually, eventually to purify themselves to such a degree that they could enter into Hierarchical circles and serve Them.

Hierarchy has a Plan, and this Plan is built around the Purpose of the life that is ensouling our planet. There is an Architect that knows why He created this earth, why He created this humanity, this whole life. There is a Purpose in His mind. This Purpose is sealed and covered. We cannot see it. You ask yourself, "What is the purpose of life? Why was I born," especially when you are sick and in the hospital. You ask, "Why was I born? What is this all about?" Sometimes, even in great pleasures, you suddenly awaken and say, "What is the purpose of this?" This awakening is a great question which makes you search for the Purpose that exists in all our

136

solar system. You may ask, Why was this solar system created? What is the purpose? How can we realize and actualize that purpose?

The Hierarchy, through meditation and advanced teaching, slowly, slowly penetrates into this Purpose to understand what the Boss wants. For example, the Boss wants our souls to graduate and eventually, eventually become Divine, spotless, pure, all-knowing, all-feeling, all-seeing perfection as human beings.

Let us say that this is the Purpose of that Great Lord. Now how can this Purpose be achieved? Hierarchy formulates and decides what humanity must do to actualize this Purpose. So in thinking and working to realize the Purpose, the outcome is a Plan. Hierarchy has a Plan, and if you follow that Plan, you can reach the Purpose.

What is the Plan? The Plan is both very easy and very difficult, but we can make it simple. The Plan is that every human being, even every animal, every bird, every bush, every flower be enlightened. This is the first step of the Plan. So Hierarchy decides, formulates the ways and means of how to make humanity enlightened. "Let Light descend on earth." In illumination, when it comes to your mind, first, you see who and what you are. Second, you see who you want to be. Third, you see what the ways are to become what you want to be.

The first part of the Plan is the illumination of all humanity. When the light comes, you can see yourself. "I am a crook. I am a thief. I am a liar. I am a materialist. I am a greedy dog. I am this or that." You can see it. You cannot hide what you really are from the light. Socrates said, "Know thyself." You can see yourself, but you can hide from yourself. You can say you are not that, but you know that you are that.

First, illumination comes to your mind, and you see what you are. This is a terrible thing. It is really terrible. You do not understand yet, but once you see in the clear light of day what you are, you will be terrified of yourself, what you made yourself. That is a difficult test to pass. Sometimes people see that they are a monkey, and they run away from the monkey. They take a bottle of whiskey and drink it. They fall into pleasures and try to forget themselves. They try to do everything to forget themselves because they do not like to see themselves as a monkey with a big tail. Sometimes they cannot escape themselves. This is very psychological. I am making it comical, but it is very psychological.

Sometimes they do not run from themselves. Instead, they identify with themselves and say, "I am a monkey. I am a liar. I am a greedy man. I am a materialist. I am a jealous person. I hate people." They accept what they are. Once they accept what they are, they become what they accept. They mold it and become that. They crystallize within their own image. It is very difficult to save them from themselves. When you see yourself as a monkey and you accept it, you cannot separate from the monkey. This is a very psychological problem. We cannot make people separate from "themselves" and see the reality that they are not monkeys, that they are higher beings. How do we separate people from that with which they are cemented, when they have become one, become identified with their false self?

The second part of illumination is you see what you desire or want to become. Through your own efforts or with outer help, detach yourself from the monkey and try to identify yourself with some self-image that is more healthy, more fitting, more beautiful, more harmonious with your inner desires or visions, if you can. To improve yourself you can study the lives of people who served humanity by living a heroic or beautiful life.

The third point of illumination is to see the ways by which you can become whatever you want to be. This is where starts your intelligent planning and following your plan step by step to illuminate yourself through books or a teacher or in meditation or in service. Eventually you will find ways and means to illuminate yourself and achieve that which you want to be.

The second part of the Plan is a little deeper. You must imagine that universities, colleges, higher education, and so on are in the Plan. The second part of the Plan is Love. "Let all men Love." It is a Plan which for twenty million years we have been working on, yet we have not accomplished much. Still we kill each other, still we hate each other, still we are jealous of each other, and love is not here. Our love is mostly a lie. There are a few people who love each other, who are ready to sacrifice for each other, who try to elevate each other, to evoke creativeness and greatness from each other. That is love. Look how beautiful it is. The Plan is Light and Love and the creation of universal harmony, cooperation, and under-standing. Hierarchy takes that Light and Love and prepares the designs, the blueprints, of how Love must be achieved. It is not easy. It takes thousands and millions of years to make humanity understand that love is more beneficial and health-bringing than hate, than jealousy, than revenge. It is difficult because people are identified with their "monkey." Hierarchy is trying to educate people to love each other, to respect each other, to identify with each other. Why is that? It is because the One Self is within us. We are respecting and loving the One Self that is within us. That is the second part of the Plan.

The third part of the Plan is to increase the Will in humanity. The will is direction; the will is the energy of actualization. People say for example, "I want to be beauti-ful," and they become beautiful. They do not wait anymore because they have willpower. "I do not want to smoke any-more." The next minute they do not smoke because the energy is there. "I want to lose weight," and they lose weight. "I want to have weight," and they have weight because they have willpower. Willpower is the energy of actualization. Whatever you put into your vision, you become the vision itself, through your willpower.

The Hierarchy is working in these three fields and making a Plan, "Let the Plan of Light and Love work out, and may it seal the door where evil dwells." It is fantastic. We are going into Light, Love, and Will energy. Why? It is so we eliminate all hindrances from humanity which make life miserable.

Hierarchy has no limitations of time and space in Their consciousness. They are scattered all over the world. Actually, there are two members of Hierarchy in the United States. There is one in Russia, one in Canada, two in India, two or three in Egypt. They are scattered but are continuously in telepathic communication. For Them there is no time and space. They communicate telepathically, and They make Their decisions. Once or twice a year They collectively sit together and decide the next phase of the Plan. These children learned A. Then what next, B. They learned B, then C and D and F, and so on. Hierarchy is the educational center of this planet. They work and act in the energy, in the vortex, of love. There is nothing for Them except love. They are the Center of Love. As humanity thinks about these Centers, the Centers influence humanity. Now I feel They are feeling that we are talking about Them, and Their energies are spreading to us. You individually must think about Hierarchy because Hierarchy is the only way that our salvation is accomplished.

It is said in many books that Hierarchy made calls to human beings to "help Us." We must be helpers to Hierarchy to lessen Their burdens. It is not that God is sitting there hallucinating and angels are dancing around Him singing psalms and everything is okay. They are serving the whole world. They are not only serving the whole world but also are serving human beings in the astral, mental, and spiritual levels. These four levels are Their field of service. The Great Sage, in one of

His verses, says very beautifully, "Sometimes in Our labor Our sweat drops as big drops of blood." That is how hard They work to help humanity. If Their help was not with us we would, in ten years, eat each other like cannibals. This is the human downfall. The Hierarchy is helping to elevate cultures and civilizations with laws, regulations, great inspiration, and illumination. They are helping all humanity, step-by-step, to go forward. If They cut their relationship from us, we will turn into animals, hating each other, killing each other, and finishing each other off. That is what the moon humanity did. On the moon, Hierarchy withdrew Its help because humanity was obnoxious, and within one hundred, two hundred years they destroyed each other, they bombed each other, they annihilated each other, and the moon turned into ashes. If the Hierarchy enters into your brain and heart, you feel that you have direction, you have support, you have a refuge to go somewhere, to be something.

THE GREAT INVOCATION

From the point of Light within the Mind of God
Let light stream forth into the minds of men.
Let Light descend on Earth.

From the point of Love within the Heart of God
Let love stream forth into the hearts of men.
May Christ return to Earth.

From the centre where the Will of God is known
Let purpose guide the little wills of men —
The purpose which the Masters know and serve.

From the centre which we call the race of men
Let the Plan of Love and Light work out
And may it seal the door where evil dwells.

Let Light and Love and Power restore the Plan on earth.

16

TRUE SERVICE TO HIERARCHY

Let us see how people understand Service to the Lord and Hierarchy. He who thinks of ascending only by prayer is far from Service. He who in his labor hopes to bring the best efforts for the welfare of humanity must adopt the Lord with his heart. He who does not relinquish his own comfort does not know how to serve Hierarchy. He who does not accept the Indications of the Hierarchy does not understand Service. Only when the heart is ready to accept consciously the affirmation sent by the Highest Will can it be said that the realization of Service is adopted. Thus, we are no lovers of funereal rites and of empty invocations of the Lord. Thus, we venerate the striving of disciples to the Service of Hierarchy. Hence, it is so easy to observe how the one who does not accept the Service in spirit venerates the Lord and Hierarchy so long as the way is convenient to him.

Thus, We take into account each effort to remove the burden from the Hierarchy; as in the great, so in the small. Thus, in Our creativeness, We affirm reverence not in words but by deeds. Thus, We deplore it when We see reverence in words but not in actions.

Hierarchy, para. 295
Agni Yoga Society

Let us see how people understand service to the Lord and Hierarchy. How do you understand service to the Lord? Are you serving first to the Lord? Who is the Lord? You say, "I have my steak, my radio, my beer, my sex. I am enjoying it. Who is the Lord?" The Lord is not present, and Hierarchy is not present. You can serve to the Lord by loving each other, by respecting each other highly, by humiliating yourself to raise each other up, by inspiring each other with Goodness, Righteousness, Beauty, by making each other strive. You buy books and spread them. You give lectures. You create angels from human beings; you create efficient, intelligent people, so that they cooperate with each other and create movements and organizations that will serve humanity in achieving happiness, health, and prosperity. It is not an abstraction. You must achieve health. Every time you are healing somebody, or helping to heal somebody, you are serving the Lord because in that man nothing exists except the Lord. That is how you are going to see each other.

"Oh, so and so is crazy. So and so is dirty. So and so is very beautiful. So and so is very rich." It is not so and so. It is only one Lord living within you. This is the thing which you must achieve. To achieve it you are going to destroy millions of barriers, millions of thoughtforms, millions of inherited emotions, traditions, and so on. You are going to clean it from your mind. When the computer is clean, it takes new programming. You program yourself to believe that the Lord is in you, and in His Life you live. In "Him we live and move and have our being." If that Lord evaporates, we are a trash bag. Nothing else exists but Him. This is the basis of all civil laws, rules, and regulations, but people do not see it. From these higher concepts came our laws, as far as we were able to understand them.

How are you serving Hierarchy? To serve Hierarchy means to understand Their Plan, to teach Their Plan, and to work for Their Plan. For example, you have a million dollars. You keep it in the bank, you bury it, you die like a donkey, and money goes to various places. The money did not help you.

Today you are alive. Put your money into those organizations and activities that are serving Hierarchy. Put your energy there. Put your mind there. Serve Hierarchy. If you serve Hierarchy, you are taking Their burdens. They need millions and millions of people to work. There are sixty-six members of Hierarchy now on the planet. Everyone who becomes a Third Degree Initiate becomes a member of the Hierarchy. They teach him, then make him a Fourth Degree Initiate, a Fifth Degree Initiate, a Sixth Degree Initiate. Eventually he becomes somebody in humanity and in Hierarchy. Your intention is to be somebody. In humanity you shine with your wisdom. With your creativity you radiate.

What is creativity? You create all those steps that are taking humanity to the Hierarchical level, to enlighten them, to make them really love each other, to be really active, and to be creative. In this way you are helping Hierarchy. Then Hierarchy is not sending Its Masters to come and talk to the group because the group now has a few people who can speak, people who can lead. In this way you serve Them by saving Their time, energy, and lifting Their burden. You take Their burdens on your shoulders. Do not ask, "God, give me a new car. God, give me a new girlfriend." Okay, have them, but then what? What are you giving to God? That is what the Hierarchy demands, that you penetrate into It and say, "Lord, I think I am ready." They will ask, "How are you ready?" "My body is healthy. My emotions are pure, inclusive, and all-embracing. My mind is sharp and clear. I can think in the light of Your

Beauty, Goodness, Truth. My personality is educated and disciplined and has every kind of subtle, harmonious, and beautiful etiquette. Now I think I am ready. Can I serve You?" They say, "Good, good, good. You come here," and They send you to the most obnoxious places in the world to try out your vision, energy, and purpose. You succeed, and then They elevate you, slowly, slowly making you work in the places where They need your prayers, your blessings, your light, your love, and your willpower. Now you have entered into the first degree of Hierarchical service.

Yesterday I saw a man. He brought me a manuscript. It was intellectual, academic, sophisticated. I called him back. I asked, "What is this?" He replied, "This is an academic paper, an intellectual paper. This is what is accepted in universities and colleges." I said, "This is not worth one penny. There is no love in it; there is no light in it; there is no willpower; there is no actualization; there is no direction; there is no Hierarchy; there is no compassion. What is this? You are kidding yourself. It is academic gymnastics. See the suffering of humanity. See their pain and actually serve them." That is Hierarchical direction.

He who thinks of ascending only by prayer is far from Service. You sit in the chair and pray and pray. What do you pray for? You say, "Give me shoes, give me pants, give me success, kill my enemies, massacre them, and I want a girlfriend." You do not pray for other things such as, "Make me to see myself." You do not say, "Lord, if I am not in line, bring me in line." He brings you in line, and you hate God because you are in line. You sing psalms and prayers and say, "I am serving God." I went to a prayer meeting once. Fifty people were praying. I went crazy. What are you praying for? Say, "God, show me how I can help You." This is the prayer. "Show me the ways and means by which I can help You," not "give something to me."

146

He who in his labor hopes to bring the best efforts for the welfare of humanity must adopt the Lord with his heart. If you want to help, everything you do physically, in your business, in your conversation, in your relationships, on your vacations must be a part of the service for the Hierarchy, for the good of humanity. Whatever I am doing, whatever I am saying, whatever I am feeling, whatever I am thinking, whatever my life is as a whole, is it helping toward the good of humanity? But to do that you must be one in your heart with the Lord. You must feel your oneness with Him.

He who does not relinquish his own comfort does not know how to serve Hierarchy. The first thing people like is "my comfort" — in the car, in the railway station, in the boats, in the parties, in the dancing — "my comfort." In your business, in your creative actions, it is "my comfort." If you cannot renounce or relinquish yourself from your comforts and accept pain, suffering, agony, battle, striving, and effort, you cannot serve Hierarchy. Why? It is because all these things prepare your muscles to be in Hierarchical service. "I found my wife. My wife has so much money, and collectively we have two, three million dollars. I will sit down and start snoring and be happy. The hell with everything else." But then suddenly you hear in your ear, "Tomorrow your soul will be taken. What benefit do you have?" You must always live in the light of death. I did not say "in the fear of death" but "in the light of death" that tomorrow, maybe in half an hour, you are not here anymore. You will not be here twenty-five years later, ten years later, maybe five years later, so pack, arrange yourself, and think about the journey you are going to make.

Those who cannot relinquish their comfort cannot serve humanity. Comfort must be crushed if you want to serve. The Great Sage says that "sometimes We go to the cities for service, but every night We change our habitat so that people do not find Us, do not see Us." They are uncomfortable every minute for the sake of helping the good of humanity. It is so beautiful. Do not be comfortable too much. Get busy, work, do something because the life is going. The life is not going to stay there. I saw it when they took me to the hospital. I said to myself, "You are going." Then God said, "Let him stay a little more to suffer." I said, "I will do that." It is very interesting. When you have the light of death in your consciousness, you behave. You turn to the Hierarchy.

Life as a whole is suffering, is pain, is destruction, is war. What else do you have? In Europe, they are killing each other. In the Middle East, they are butchering each other. In South Africa, they are doing the same thing. The situation is boiling. For what is this pot boiling? It is to cook the "pilaf." The "pilaf" is enlightenment. The "pilaf" is to love each other and help each other. That is the "pilaf" that we must eat. This is very important for us.

A man came to Christ. Christ asked, "Why did you not come yesterday to the meeting?" The man said, "My father died and I buried him." Christ asked another man, "Why did you not come to the meeting?" "Oh, I was marrying." "Why did you not come to the meeting?" "I was watching television." "Why did you not come to the meeting?" "I had business transactions. I was signing a contract." "Why did you not come to the meeting?" "I was loving my wife." "Ah," He asked, "This is what discipleship is? This is what membership is? Go, I do not want to see you because you are busy with the things that do not lead you to life. You are busy with the things that lead you to death, to destruction." That is the message.

He who does not accept the Indications of the Hierarchy does not understand Service. What is the indication of the Hierarchy? It is written about in *The Externalisation of the Hierarchy, Initiation, Human and Solar,* and in *Supermundane,* Volumes I and II, and in great events that we witness. For example, suddenly a nation is destroyed. We saw a great event in this century. After seventy years a most powerful nation collapsed. How did it happen? It was because of corruption. If they were in the Hierarchical line, they would be a super, super power. They cheated, they killed, they destroyed each other underneath. They destroyed people. They manipulated the world. There was no moral basis. Moral basis is the Hierarchical Plan. If you are destroying people, you cannot survive. The moral basis evaporated, and if the foundation is gone, down goes all the rest. Indications you can see, but indications are different for you. For example, you have a feeling that you must help, that you must teach, that you must dedicate yourself, that you must offer, that you must sacrifice. These indications come to you, and you listen or do not listen.

Once I was invited to an organization to help raise money. I did not know the organization, but I said I would do my best because they believed that I could do something. I spoke very well. I explained to the people what was needed. That day we collected forty thousand dollars. There were eighty or ninety people. A lady looked at me and took out her checkbook. She started writing, then stopped and closed her checkbook. "Lady," I said, "do not let Satan hold your hand." It is very psychological, very dramatic. She had an *indication* that she must help, and in that help another influence came saying, "Do not help." Satan held her hand. So *indications* are many: some emotions, some inspirations, some impressions, some telepathic messages, some feelings that you must do something. Do it. If you do not follow this indication, other indications do not come to you anymore.

Only when the heart is ready to accept consciously the affirmation sent by the Highest Will can it be said that the realization of Service is adopted. The form of service, in essence, is given to us by the Highest Will. When we are ready in our heart and consciously engage ourselves in that service, then we feel that our service is affirmed by the Hierarchy.

Thus, we are no lovers of funereal rites and of empty invocations of the Lord. The Hierarchy cannot be impressed by anything that is superficial. It must come from all our being and heart if we want the Hierarchy to accept it.

Thus, we venerate the striving of disciples to the Service of Hierarchy. Veneration means that They send energy and help us to fulfill our obligations in service.

Hence, it is so easy to observe how the one who does not accept the Service in spirit venerates the Lord and Hierarchy so long as the way is convenient to him. If one cannot accept service in spirit, how can he venerate the Lord and the Hierarchy? Only by service can we express our respect and love to the Lord and the Hierarchy. Many people, staying in comfort, think that they are serving the Hierarchy, whereas they are only doing things that are convenient for them to do.

Thus, We take into account each effort to remove the burden from the Hierarchy; as in the great, so in the small. The Hierarchy takes account of all actions which are taken to remove the burden from the Hierarchy, no matter if their service is small or great. Even a cup of water given to a thirsty man is observed. Even a few comforting words to a suffering man is considered. There is no big and small service. Only the motive behind the service is important. All that we do must be done for the service of the Lord. Even if you write a letter with all your heart, it is a service. Many people try to help people quit smoking, doping, and so on. This is a service. Still higher service is to clean people's glamors, illusions, hatreds, and fears.

Thus, in Our creativeness, We affirm reverence not in words but by deeds. The creativeness of the Hierarchy is to serve the manifold needs of humanity. Every help given is a creative process which evokes the urge to overcome difficulties and to pave the way for future advancement.

Thus, we deplore it when We see reverence in words but not in actions. Hierarchy is a center of positive actions to serve humanity and lower kingdoms.

Question: If I see myself as a monkey with a big tail, you say that I am doomed because I accept that of myself. Do you also think that you have to see yourself as you are in order to go to the next step?

Answer: There are two sides. I said only one side of it. If you see that you are a monkey, if you attach to that monkey, and you decide to live as a monkey, you can do that individually, or society as a whole can do that. It is very difficult to separate that monkey from your Real Self. You need psychological, educational, religious, and spiritual discipline so that you take that monkey and bury it and emancipate yourself.

The other side is that you can identify with the angel within you. You have an angel. You identify with that angel. You strive to be that angel, and you live among society as a benevolent energy, as a source of beauty, righteousness, creativity. That is the second side of it. With which side are you identifying your-self — monkey side or angel side? You can detach yourself from the monkey by reading, meditating, and seeing a different image than you have. You can even go to the past and see when you were identified with your angel, and you strengthen that identifi-cation so that you weaken the identification with the monkey. In this way you can elevate yourself, but you must have a teacher, you must have friends who are on the path of relinquishing their monkeys and becoming human beings.

Identifying with your "angel" or visions or ideal is also very dangerous in the sense that you lose your normality or equilibrium, your sense of proportion. Sometimes your body, your emotions, your mind are devastated in actualizing your "ideal" in the society and in the times in which you live.

Identification with the ideal requires a gradual process, and, with each step, actualization must be demonstrated. If this is not done, suddenly you find that many bridges on the path do not exist, and you cannot be normal or go to your ideal nature.

The ideal eats you, devours you, and you become an "ideal" who stands in the streets and shouts, "I am the Messiah," or someone who starts activities to prove he is somebody without having a foundation. These are mental diseases and need to be handled wisely.

On the other hand, identification with the monkey makes you a "monkey" and does not let you grow, or the monkey in you becomes the source of endless trouble in society.

These three vehicles are in one nature, as for example we say, "Father, Son, and Holy Spirit." These are three aspects of one God. We can also say that these three aspects are in one manifestation, but they function in different evolutionary stages and finally become one. They synthesize.

The Great Sage says,

In the mighty shifting of nations what can be the saving manifestation? What else can provide the direction to the Good if not the way toward Hierarchy? When the spirit of humanity sinks into the lower strata, what can bring it to the higher understanding if not adherence to Hierarchy?. . .[1]

Question: The Hierarchy is building a Plan, the application of which we achieve some understanding of the Purpose of Shamballa. Is this right?

Answer: It is. The Hierarchy takes the currents of energy from Shamballa and interprets them for us and translates them for humanity. Actually, the Plan is the translation of the Purpose for humanity. The Hierarchy takes part of the Purpose, which has immediate relation to our cycle and evolution, and builds a Plan in the intuitive substance. Thus, the

---

1. Agni Yoga Society, *Hierarchy*, para. 441

Plan is substantial and highly tangible for those whose consciousness functions in the Intuitional Plane.

Each part of the Plan can be translated in seven ways to meet the needs of the seven fields of human labor. Each part of the Plan is synthesized and its application leads us into synthesis of these seven fields.

Thus, one can say that the purpose of the Plan is to create synthesis by the application of new ideas of progress in all seven fields.

17

VANGUARDS OF HUMANITY

"The existence of Hierarchy is the foundation of the entire life."[1]

"It can easily be seen how the followers of the Hierarchy were enriched with true values."[2]

". . . the anchor for salvation is the focus of Hierarchy."[3]

Sometimes you must read these words and learn them by heart so that you repeat them in your consciousness because as you repeat these words in your consciousness, audibly or inaudibly, it penetrates into your bones. Then it penetrates into your consciousness, and then it goes to your higher consciousness, and eventually it controls and illuminates your life. That is why they say sometimes to learn a few phrases and repeat them. For example, there was a lady who was always depressed for some reason. I said, "Always repeat the mantram 'More

1. Agni Yoga Society, *Hierarchy*, para. 212
2. *Ibid.*, para. 266
3. *Ibid.*, para. 315

Radiant than the Sun.'" When she did this for one, two months, she was able to control her depression.

Esoterically, the word "Hierarchy" means the group of Initiates who dedicated Their life to improve human conditions and lead humanity toward perfection. If you see people or leaders or saints or sages whose prime intention is to improve life, not only in one area, not only in two areas, but in all areas, so that people feel happy, healthy, prosperous, enlightened, and progressive, then they are Initiates.

Initiates are those Who are always improving Their life. That is what initiation means. If you have a consciousness which is one yard, when it becomes two yards you are an Initiate. If you are understanding life one percent and suddenly you start understanding life ninety percent, you are an Initiate. You are also an Initiate when you slowly start seeing how backward you are, the failures you have, how you are defeating yourself and your purpose in the life. That is also expansion of consciousness because if your consciousness is not expanded, you can see yourself as a king, as a queen, as a great sage, but once the light increases in you, you see yourself exactly as you are.

This is very important for each one of us because on the path of the Hierarchy we cannot carry with us the trash that we are or have. Every minute that trash must be dumped, and we must get rid of the trash which loads us physically, emotionally, and mentally. Initiates are those people who continuously get rid of the imperfections or hindrances which they have in their nature. They are those who are overcoming their limitations and enlightening themselves. Thus slowly, slowly they become part of the Hierarchy.

Members of the Hierarchy are the fruits of evolution. Hierarchy is based on the Law of Spiritual Evolution. Our essence gains experience, knowledge, and illumination as days and years and lives pass. For example, when you were fifteen years old, you did many things. Then later you realized that some of them were wrong. Now you are realizing that you should not repeat them. In the past you had a little experience, for example, in marriage, in leadership, in many, many fields of human labor. You had a few experiences, but as the years passed, your experience increased, your knowledge deepened, the field of your enlightenment expanded. If all these are repeated over twenty years, fifty years, seventy years, seventy lives, five hundred lives, your life becomes so rich. Your knowledge is accumulated in your soul, just like in a computer, and you become a source of knowledge, experience, and guidance.

You have enlightenment when you see yourself and life exactly as they are. This is enlightenment. It does not come suddenly, as if you enter into the light and become radioactive. Enlightenment is gradual and cumulative. You start to see your face, your heart, your mind, your intentions, your motivations as they are. When you see them as they are, you have a different kind of enlightenment. After seeing yourself, you start seeing others. That is very important because if you start seeing others before you start seeing yourself, you become critical, slanderous, prideful, and so on.

It is very interesting that most of humanity thinks other than what they are, thinks differently than what they are. They think they are doctors, they are lawyers, they are healers, and so on. But if you shake them and really see their essence, you can find nothing there or very little. That something is their real being or what they are exactly, physically, emotionally, mentally, which they are going to find. Unless one finds out what he is, there is no progress for him. This is because what you are is the foundation upon which you build your future. What you are not is like sand upon which you build your mansion, and it falls down eventually.

The first essential step is to endeavor to be a part of the

Hierarchy through enlightenment. Be enlightened about others. Increase your knowledge and especially your experience. Knowledge is not experience. You can know how this machine works, but when I tell you to repair it, you cannot repair it. Experience is a little higher than knowledge. Sometimes even experience replaces knowledge. Those who are on the path going toward Hierarchy are people who, year after year, life after life, cycle after cycle are increasing their illumination, their knowledge, and their experience. When this continues year after year, in comparison with those people who are not striving, you become a giant. These giants are the members of the Hierarchy.

For example, you have a school-age child who is just learning the ABCs of mathematics. Then you have Einstein, Edison, Tesla, Marconi, and Great Ones, who are masters in comparison to these children. A time will come when eventually you will see yourself in relative maturity, which people call perfection. There is no ultimate maturity in the Universe. Maturity is all relative. Even if you become a Master and you start looking toward the Universe, you feel just like a baby. But we have degrees of maturity for which you are going to prepare yourself.

These experiences, knowledge, and illumination are multiplied if we do not waste our time and energy with nonessentials, but live and labor for the most essential. Of course, life puts us in conditions and situations in which, whether we like it or not, we learn. You learn from your failures, from your defeats, from books, from universities, from your teacher, from your friends, from your mommy and daddy, and so on. You learn, but it is a forceful learning.

What is the best way of learning? First, slowly, slowly eliminate from your life all those actions which are wasting your time because they are non-essential, and second, focus your life slowly, slowly on the most essential. For example, a man was working in a high position. When he was sixty-five he asked, "What am I doing? Day and night, eight hours, ten hours, fifteen hours I am wasting my time for a little money, for a little company." Eventually he resigned and he focused his whole attention, his whole labor on how to perfect himself and serve people. He chose the way leading to the most essential.

In your life you will find millions of both non-essentials and essentials, but when you start dedicating your life to the most essential, that is the moment when you assimilate your experiences, your knowledge, your illumination, and you become a part of the Hierarchy.

If you really love yourself, you are going to work for the most essential. For example, you have 500 bottles of water. Most of them are polluted, but one or two of them are not polluted. If you love yourself, do not be in a hurry to go and drink polluted water. You wait a little. Discriminate and choose the bottle which has pure water. When you find the bottle which is pure, drink it. This is discrimination. Also you may do this with your thoughts. Which thoughts are really nice, beneficial, pure, clean, beautiful, and which are not? You choose really pure thoughts, pure emotions, pure actions, pure and beautiful relationships. What are you doing? You are discriminating and discovering the most essential in your life. When you lose the most essential and you start running after non-essentials, you commit a crime against the Law of Economy.

Your time, your energy, your life are treasures, and if you are wasting your life, your energy, your mind, your heart, your body, it means you do not love yourself. In a correct understanding, you must love yourself but not at the expense of others. You must love yourself so that you guide yourself in the right direction. When you love yourself, you do all that is possible to make your body healthy, your emotions pure, and your mind creative. How can you love yourself if you let these three bodies act against your progress? You want to take care of your body because you love your body. You want to take care of your heart and mind because if you lose your heart and mind, you have lost everything. If you lose your heart, you have lost your life. You take care of these things because you love them, and when you love them your past experiences, enlightenment, and knowledge are used to lead your body, emotions, and mind into the right direction.

Those who strive and reach deeper experience, knowledge, and illumination become the teachers and leaders of humanity. This is so obvious. Some people are just like cattle. Some people are leading the cattle. We have cowboys who are leading the cattle. What beautiful scenery it is to see the cowboys leading the cattle. They lead the cattle because they became human. They are not part of the cattle now. There are others who own the cowboys and cattle. You are going to move forward so that you do not sit there, but you lead the cattle. How do you lead the cattle? When you increase your knowledge, illumination, and experiences, whether you like it or not, you become a leader by the fact of your knowledge, experience, and illumination. Even if you do not have any group or people to talk and relate to, your mind radiates leadership, which means to provide light, love, and energy so that others move forward. This is leadership.

When we say "leadership," we understand it to mean a man standing in front of an army saying, "Right, left, forward." We have that type of leadership. Even that leadership is precious because one graduates from the ranks of the soldiers and becomes a leader there. Then he becomes a sergeant and so on. Leadership is based on assimilating your knowledge, experience, and illumination.

People must know about the Hierarchy. I know some of you have heard about the Hierarchy. In comparison with the animal kingdom, you are the Hierarchy. In comparison to the Hierarchy, we are cattle. In comparison to the galactic

Hierarchy, our Hierarchy is like first grade. There is a ladder which we are climbing, and this ladder must be climbed if we want to bring Beauty, Goodness, Righteousness, Joy, and Freedom to humanity. Do you see how beautiful it is when our children, from the beginning, realize that they are precious, that they have lots of resources: physical, emotional, mental, money, and position resources, and that these resources must be used for the most essential? The most essential is to be a leader to guide humanity, to improve life, to heal diseases, to eliminate pollution. That is the Hierarchical job. The Hierarchical job is not to go to the Himalayas and live in caves. Everyone who is doing a great job of improving life and the lives of people is a part and member of the Hierarchy. Have a little more confidence in yourself and a greater appreciation for yourself because you have already graduated from the mineral and vegetable kingdoms. You are not a cabbage anymore. You came from the animal kingdom. Who knows what animals we were. Eventually, we graduated and initiated into the human kingdom. Here we see exactly what was our past and what our future can be.

The members of the Hierarchy are those individuals who throughout millions of years went ahead and became the vanguards of humanity. They are not some mysterious people who appear and disappear or live here and there. They are real vanguards which means authorities — authorities in the political field, in the educational field, in the field of communication, science, art, religion, and finance. They are graduated authorities. For example, if you ask, "What can we do to change education?""and you have a contact with the Hierarchy, the educational department of the Hierarchy will enlighten your mind and say, "Education in the United States and education in the world are great failures. Do this, this, this, to change the situation." They are authorities, but They do not impose Their knowledge and experience and illumination upon us. They want us to grow and to be able to communicate with Them so that They give Their knowledge, experience, and illumination to us.

What is Their knowledge and experience based upon? Their knowledge and experience is based upon Their millions of years of labor. They are doing the job and learning it. They are suffering, They are dedicating, They are sacrificing themselves. Eventually, They are maturing. They wait for us to go and take Their gift. Actually, Their entire radiation and thought-forms, Their intentions and plans are floating in space because *They think.* Whenever you think, you broadcast your thought automatically. It is so important to know this. Whenever you think, you broadcast your knowledge, your thought, your interpretation, your plan, your intention, your motives into space. If you build your psychic radio or antenna, you will pick them up. Why? Ideas, visions, and great knowledge do not belong to us. They are in space. We bring them down, focus them into writings, into music, into leadership. They are there. People must advance through meditation, dedication, devotion, and a sacrificial life and eventually make a break-through toward that "cloud of knowledge," experience, and illumination and slowly, slowly start picking them up and bringing them down to earth.

When I was driving to Los Angeles, I was tuned to a radio station which was far away. The station had a lot of static. I said, "I want to tune into that station." Ten miles later, the static was not as heavy. Fifteen miles later, the station was clear. I learned something: As we advance toward the station of light, the station of experience, we get better messages.

You become a leader, a vanguard automatically as you increase your knowledge, your experience, and your illumination. Those who are illuminated and full of knowledge and experience never search for positions. Searching for position is a sign that you do not have that experience, that knowledge, that illumination. People will come to your feet and say, "Please come and be our leader" because you are ready, and people are looking for leaders, for the vanguards of humanity. The Hierarchy is the vanguard of humanity.

All great leaders, saints, and sages of humanity are members of the Hierarchy. Race, color, sex, nationality, religion are not taken into consideration. In the Hierarchy we are told that there are blacks, there are whites, there are yellows of all religions, of all races, of all nationalities, of all sexes. Sometimes people think that when we talk about the Masters, we are talking about men. There are many women in the Hierarchy. You can see in the world how women are making breakthroughs and reaching higher and higher positions. But who are these people who are reaching higher positions? They are those who to some degree are choosing the most essential in life, instead of wasting their time on non-essentials.

Hierarchy is divided into seven main groups, which we call Ashrams. In each group you can find a highly elevated being. In humanity we have seven fields of human endeavor which correspond to these seven Ashrams: politics, education, communication, art, science, religion, and finance. These seven Ashrams are powerhouses, radio stations, which every minute radiate thoughts and guidance to humanity through these seven fields. Those in these seven fields who are sensitive to Their thoughts and directions bring changes into their respective fields.

If you had ten people in the government who were really focused on the Hierarchy, the real politics would start dawning. They would think, "Why are we here? What is our position? What is our duty and responsibility?" Hierarchy is here. The treasure house is here. Only you are going to approach Hierarchy and make yourself super-sensitive to receiving clearly, telepathically, Their guidance. After you receive the ideas from Hierarchy, you are going to ask, "Can I really apply all these ideas in my environment? What is the political and economic situation; what are the difficulties and hindrances; what are the opposing forces that may react if I start something that humanity is not ready to assimilate?"

How do you approach Hierarchy? How do you get closer to the Hierarchy? The most important thing is purification — purification of your mind and heart. And thus, slowly, you approach Hierarchy.

The seven groups of Hierarchy each have subsidiary groups, or sub-Ashrams, forming an entity of forty-nine Ashrams. Sub-Ashrams have a Fifth Degree Initiate. A Fifth Degree Initiate is a man or a woman Who is consciously immortal. He or She cannot die anymore. He or She may or may not live in a physical body.

There are also those Who are called the Three Heads of the Hierarchy. They coordinate the whole labor of the Hierarchy. One of Them is called the Manu, another is the Christ, and the third one is called the Lord of Civilization. The Manu works on the First Ray, the Christ works on the Second Ray of Love-Wisdom, and the Lord of Civilization works on the Third, Fourth, Fifth, Sixth, and Seventh Rays. In reality, the entire Hierarchy is the Ashram of that Great Being Who is called the Lord of Shamballa.

In each of the seven major Ashrams there is a Chohan, One Who is so far advanced that His knowledge, experience, and enlightenment have started to penetrate beyond this planet. From that high position He looks down in deep compassion to this life and thinks, "How much life must be changed, how this pollution must be purified, how this animosity and hatred and fear in humanity must be cleaned."

I was watching television and the announcer said that in Europe the rain came and flooded many, many fields and many, many cities with radioactive pollution. The fields that

were covered with water will not produce fruit, will not produce vegetables for many, many years, or if they do grow, they
will be polluted. What are we doing? How do we start to clean
up the pollution? How can we stop the fumes coming from the
factories and cars? We are in a trap. If you stop the cars, millions of people would not have a salary. If they do not have a
salary, crime will increase. We caught ourselves and put ourselves in a trap and are thinking, how do we escape from the
trap? We cannot break it with our own thinking. We need the
help of the Hierarchy.

If you elevate yourself toward the Hierarchy, They will
give you the ways and means by which you may escape that
trap. Those higher beings who are beyond our planetary
knowledge and experience and illumination know better than
we do. In thinking about Hierarchy, in focusing yourself on
Hierarchy, you really prepare your life to be beneficent for
humanity.

*At the head of each Ashram we have a Master, a Fifth
Degree Initiate, and a substitute for that Initiate.* For example, in Alice A. Bailey's case the sub-ashram was the Tibetan
Master's Ashram, and Alice Bailey, though alive, was working
in this higher realm as a substitute for the Tibetan Master.

Question: There are seven major Ashrams and seven under
each one. What are the responsibilities of the seven under the
seven?

Answer: The seven major Ashrams direct the work of their
corresponding sub-Ashrams. There is something very beautiful here. Each major Ashram works on one of the Seven Rays,
and each major Ashram is divided into seven, which means
that the certain Ray under which the Ashram works is divided
into seven sub-Rays through its members Who are used to
meeting the various needs in the sub-Ashrams.

Every major Ashram has a department that is dedicated to
human progress and human welfare and a department that

receives impressions from Shamballa and gives to Hierarchy, so that They in turn give to humanity. The seven fields are politics, education, communication, the arts, science, religion, and finance.

For example, there are financiers there. Who are the financiers? They are those Masters Who worked with money, with the economy for hundreds of lives. What do you expect from them? Their computer is full of programs. They are ready to tell you what to do, what not to do. This country, that country, this city, that city is becoming bankrupt, which is the failure of economics, the failure of people who are working in that field. Whenever you have a failure, as a human instinct you say, "I was not successful because of this or that condition, because of that situation," but you never say, "It is because of my ignorance."

Question: You spoke about Alice Bailey being a substitute for the Tibetan Master. Are there substitutes in the world today whom we can recognize? How can we recognize their work?

Answer: We recognize them as Christ said: "Recognize them by their own fruits." If a man comes and says, "I am a Christ," my first question is, "What did you do for humanity?" "Nothing." "Well!" Substitutes are those people who in the absence of the Masters take over. Each Ashram is a laboratory, is a workshop, with plans and purposes. There must be a leader there to direct them. When the Master is on other planets or doing something, a substitute takes over. It is a very advanced degree position. To be on the human level and, in the meantime, to have a part of your radio station, your psychic station, somewhere else is not an easy job. For example, I am talking here and in the meantime, if I am a Master, if I am a very advanced Being, I can communicate with Them at the same time.

This happens to us sometimes. While reading we think about someone or something. Our mental mechanism can be used for various jobs if we are acting as Souls. The Great Sage speaks about divisibility of spirit, meaning that you can divide your own Self and be various places in the meantime for various duties or responsibilities. There are Those Who, during their daily duties, act also on Higher Planes.

Question: If someone thinks he is a Christ, was he ever looking for the Hierarchy?

Answer: They are mentally sick, and because of the mental derangement they think they are Christ. We do not criticize them too much. We pity them. These are people who must go to psychiatric hospitals and clean themselves. Sometimes if you tell them that they are not Christ, they will die immediately because that knowledge is holding them to this life. It is a pitiful situation, but that is not the important thing. The important thing is that often we are in that situation, and we do not see it. A lady comes and says, "I have a headache." "Oh, take an aspirin," you say, and you became a doctor. Who knows? Maybe aspirin will kill her.

An Initiate is a person whose etheric and physical bodies are purified. His heart is full of compassion and harmlessness. His mind is enlightened, and all His life is dedicated to improving the life of the planet. The degree of purification, compassion, labor, and enlightenment is the degree of His initiation.

Hierarchy has three major services:

1. To illuminate the human mind and lead humanity toward cooperation through compassion
2. To build a bridge between humanity, Hierarchy, and Shamballa
3. To protect humanity from Cosmic evil and allow its soul to progress

The Hierarchy, through Its disciples and Initiates, tries to give guidance to humanity in Its seven fields of labor.

Such disciples and Initiates are sent as groups into many nations and countries to help humanity move forward. They talk about the same principles using various languages and forms, but Their message is one. In the history of humanity we see different groups of people or individuals act as groups in different countries. They write and talk about the same principles. They even make the same discoveries on their own. The Hierarchy sends Their disciples into various nations to be the yeast for all humanity.

These groups can be in any field, according to the contemporary need of the world. Some of them clear and prepare the ground, others build, and others come and use the created buildings or mechanisms. Then groups are organized and work under a set plan to ease each other's jobs. Still there are groups in every nation who correct the mistakes of past groups. Such mistakes occur because of attacks by dark forces or existing complicated conditions.

Still other groups come and draw more energy from the Hierarchy in order to make a breakthrough within the crystallizing mental, emotional, and physical forms. Historians will have fun studying such a group phenomenon.

The Hierarchy tries to promote Its disciples into Ashrams so that they become more prepared for the service of the future. The promotion often occurs at the full moon, especially in the Taurus full moon.[4] Humanity has more and more need for Great Servers as its problems increase in volume and intensity.

Hierarchy prepares Those among Its ranks Who are ready to pass on into Shamballa, to the Father's Home, to deal with interplanetary work and problems. We are told that great ceremonies take place at the time of such events, and their influence reaches the human shore with benevolent waves.

---

4. See *Symphony of the Zodiac*, Ch. 5.

The Hierarchy on the globe is related to the greater Hierarchy existing in Sirius. Our Hierarchy receives Its direction, energy, and vision from the "White Lodge of Sirius."

Those who want to contact the Hierarchy can do so through living a life of meditation, study, sacrificial service, self-renunciation, and gratitude. These are the five steps which are always given in the Ageless Wisdom.

1. *Meditation.* Learn and do meditation every day, slowly, slowly, whether you have time or not, because meditation is one of the most essentials. Meditation is scientific thinking, balanced thinking, thinking which is based on co-measurement.

2. *Study.* Again, we have the most essential. Ask yourself, What am I reading? What are our teenagers reading? What are people reading? You are going to make a sharp discrimination in your reading because time is going, your energy is going, your brain is going, your computer is getting tired. What are you reading and studying? Sometimes we emphasize reading, to read this way, to read that way, but reading is nothing. You can read even trash. Whatever you read, are you studying it? To study means to penetrate into the ideas, into the thoughts which that book presents to you. If you found the right book and you started to study it, the proof that you are studying will be shown in the changes in your life. If your life is not changing, you are reading but not studying. You are studying but not understanding.

3. *Sacrificial service.* All of us must find ten minutes, half an hour, two hours to do a service that is really sacrificial, which means you do not expect money, praise, or flattery but come and perform a service, anywhere. Try to find a time to go and serve with selflessness, without self-interest. Such service starts opening the energy centers in your higher realms, and energy spreads into your body and life. You can experience this. Whenever you perform sacrificial service, ten minutes later you feel healthier, happier, more joyful, and free. You float in the air because you did something good. It does not matter if people praise you, appreciate you, give money to you. Just serve. The world at present needs people who are sacrificial.

I heard a report that there is a group somewhere which feeds five thousand people daily. The message emphasized the most that the leaders of that organization do not take one penny from the government. It is all public support. That is sacrificial service.

4. Self-renunciation. This is very high-level, but you can start with little amounts, ten percent, fifty percent, and reach perhaps to seventy-five percent. Renouncing yourself in practical terms means you do not feel happy when people praise you. You do not feel happy when they flatter you. You do not feel happy if they overpay you, but you continue to help people. You do not work for yourself.

Question: How is sacrificial service different from self-renunciation?

Answer: Renunciation is for yourself; sacrificial service is for others. You are going to prove that you are not really living for your sex, for your money, for your stomach, for your possessions or position. That is renunciation. Sacrificial service is all that you collected. Knowledge, illumination, experiences are going to be used for human advancement and welfare. That is the difference.

Question: What about detachment?

Answer: Detachment is sacrificial service. The progress of the human soul depends on the degree of his detachment from the objects of his limitations. These limitations have many names, such as destructive and misleading actions, negative and disturbing emotions, selfish, separative, confusing thoughts. Unless we gradually free ourselves from our crystallized habits, glamors, and illusions, we will have very slow progress during our incarnation.

To be a part of the Hierarchy is not easy, but if we succeed, the reward will be beyond our imagination. It is impossible to be a Master, a member of the Hierarchy, without mastering our life, our three bodies and their hindrances and limitations. It is not easy to master our physical limitations, but the reward is perfect health. It is not easy to master our emotional limitations, but the result is perfect joy. It is not easy to master our mental limitations, but the result is illumination.

Because of the progress of the human race, average people are fighting to master their physical limitations. Above average people are fighting to master their emotional disturbances and limitations. Advanced people are fighting to master their mental limitations and crystallizations. These are not easy tasks.

The mental equipment is very sensitive to mental currents coming from various destructive, polluted, or elevating sources. The mixture is very difficult to clean. This is why, after being able to destroy many physical and emotional hindrances, we still nourish thoughtforms which cloud our mental horizons. Extreme control is needed over our thoughts to master the mind. After that "the sound barrier" is broken; an unlimited speed in our course is open for us.

5. *Gratitude*. The Great Sage says, "People are arranged by the degree of their gratitude." How do we know that? It is so interesting. You do millions of things, and then you find that people hate you. They even slander and gossip about you. You do not mind because you are so elevated, but you feel pity for them because without gratitude they will sink into their own mire, into their own trash. Gratitude is a great sign of having health, sanity, and inner beauty.

The Hierarchy emphasizes the importance of thought, speech, and action. Through our thoughts, we may either pollute space and load it with non-essentials or charge space with new thoughtforms and beauty. Through our speech, we pollute space or we install lights in space to purify space and increase the fire in space for the use of humanity. Through our actions, we build barriers in space, create turmoil, or build communication lines in space. Through our thought, speech, and actions, we build bridges toward Higher Worlds or destroy the bridges built by others. If you want to live a victorious life in this and other worlds, think daily upon the Hierarchy, try to contact Its servers and Its members, and eventually try to be one of Them.

APPENDIX

SELECTED EXCERPTS

From Prometheus to Jesus, and from Him to the highest Adept as to the lowest disciple, every revealer of mysteries has had to become a Chrestos, a "man of sorrow" and a martyr. "Beware," said one of the greatest Masters, "of revealing the Mystery to those without"—to the profane, the Sadducee and the unbeliever. All the great Hierophants in history are shown ending their lives by violent deaths—Buddha, Pythagoras, Zoroaster, most of the great Gnostics, the founders of their respective schools; and in our own more modern epoch a number of Fire-Philosophers, of Rosicrucians and Adepts. All of these are shown—whether plainly or under the veil of allegory—as paying the penalty for the revelations they had made. This may seem to the profane reader only coincidence. To the Occultist, the death of every "Master" is significant, and appears pregnant with meaning. Where do we find in history that "messenger grand or humble, an Initiate or a Neophyte, who, when he was made the bearer of some hitherto concealed truth or truths, was not crucified and rent to shreds by the "dogs" of envy, malice and ignorance? Such is the terrible Occult law; and he who does not feel in himself the heart of a lion to scorn the savage barking, and the soul of a dove to forgive the poor ignorant fools, let him give up the Sacred Science. To succeed, the Occultist must be fearless; he has to brave dangers, dishonour and death, to be forgiving, and to be silent on that which cannot be given. Those who have vainly laboured in that direction must wait in these days—as the Book of Enoch *teaches—"until the evil-doers be consumed" and the power of the wicked annihilated. It is not lawful for the Occultist to seek or even to thirst for revenge:*

*let him wait, until sin pass away; for their [the sinners']
names shall be blotted out of the holy books [the astral
records]; their seed shall be destroyed, and their spirits slain.*

Blavatsky: *Collected Writings*, Vol. XIV, pp. 84-85.

*. . . We can affirm that each one's successful approaches to
Us over the course of centuries bears results. We know how to
be grateful; this quality of gratitude is indispensable in Our
Abode. Each affirmation of Brotherhood brings its good har-
vest. All assistance to Our Work is appreciated, and each well-
intentioned mention of the Brotherhood is remembered. In Our
Ashrams records of such good deeds are kept. We like to record
each kind smile, and Our disciples know how to rejoice at each
kind word about the Brotherhood. No one can forcibly teach
such radiant joy. No one can order gratitude. Only a broadened
consciousness can indicate where more good can be done. . . .*

Supermundane I, para. 33

*Urusvati strives to apply every hour for the General
Good; such resolve is born in the Abode, where hours are not
counted. During such a long life, can one think of hours? We
do not have earthly hours, for there are so many needs and
appeals for help from all parts of the world that it is impossible to divide Our Labor according to such relative measure-
ments. We must keep Our Consciousness in great tension in
order to be ready at each moment to send Our Will to that
place where it is most needed. Undoubtedly, We shall be
accused of sending too much help to the unworthy, and insuffi-
ciently to the deserving.*

*Those who judge by ordinary relative measures cannot
discern causes and effects. I speak not only about the tension
of labor but also about the vigilance that enables one instantly
to weigh and decide what moment and which action are the*

*most necessary. Each plea for help brings with it the emana-
tions of the past and the aroma of the future. One should blend
these harmonies in the consciousness and understand the
meaning of disharmony. We should not help a man who is
ready for evil, but must help the one who is suffering.
Contradictions may seem to conflict, but knowledge of the
past will provide the balance. Nevertheless, no plea to Us is
rejected, for by making such a request a person expresses his
recognition of the Higher World, and the fact that such a
Reality lives in space. We will not ignore a pleading voice. We
will not reject any prayer, but will gather all salutary sub-
stances in order to offer goal-fitting help. In this is contained
a special vigilance.*

*We labor constantly, and must determine Our responsi-
bility and where help is most urgently needed. Our Sister from
time immemorial has had the ability to strive constantly to the
most needed labor. Such a capacity cannot be acquired quickly,
but must be affirmed in many situations in order to become a
source of joy. This source will provide freedom from irritation,
for thought about infinite labor will produce striving without
expectation of results. There will be no thought about the past,
and in the flight forward the effects of the past will be erased.
Thus, the interplanetary whirl will stimulate vigilance and
will not disturb the joy of the broadened consciousness.*

Supermundune I, para. 34

*Urusvati has always endeavored to shorten her time in
the Subtle World. Such striving reveals a devotion to the direct
work of alleviating the suffering of humanity. If earthly people
are divided according to warmth of heart and heartlessness,
then there also exists a division between those who strive to
stay longer in the Subtle World and those who hasten toward
perfectment through reincarnation.*

We are in favor of those who hasten, despite the paradox of hastening in Infinity. We encourage all perfectment, because in it is contained the General Good. We have dedicated Ourselves to the Great Service and We summon to it all those who can help the unknown sufferers.

Our Stronghold is actually built upon this concept of help to unknown ones. Multitudes of these unknown ones who need Our care exist on Earth and in the Subtle World. Let Our Abode be called "The Great Service."

We all, at the right time, have hastened to Earth and chosen the most difficult tasks. Such conditions tempered Us and taught Us to despise persecution. The affirmers of Truth will always be persecuted by the falsifiers. No one should think that such persecutions are meant only for certain people. Every messenger of Truth must experience the onslaught of falsehood. This contact with chaos is inevitable.

You have noticed that people always place the location of Shambhala to the North. Even among the Eskimos and the Kamchatkans there exist legends about a wondrous country beyond the land of the midnight sun. The reasons for this displacement are varied. Some wanted to conceal the location of Our Abode. Some wanted to avoid the responsibility of confronting a difficult idea. Some think of their neighbors to the North as being especially fortunate. In reality it seems that all nations know about the Forbidden Country but consider themselves unworthy to have it within their boundaries!

We have a vast collection of literature on this subject. It is impossible to count the legendary heroes who are linked with Our Abode. You know about Gessar Khan and about Prester John. Everyone should understand the boundary between Truth and the popular imagination. The Abode could not have existed for so many centuries without impressing its emanations upon the people's collective memory. One should also remember

*that We are better known in the Subtle World than on Earth.
Thence come faint recollections which inspire haste in those
who have understood the significance of Great Service.*

Supermundune I, para. 51

*The district of the Gobi wilderness, and, in fact, the whole
area of Independent Tartary and Thibet is jealously guarded
against foreign intrusion. Those who are permitted to traverse
it are under the particular care and pilotage of certain agents
of the chief authority, and are duty bound to convey no intelligence respecting places and persons to the outside world. But
for this restriction, even we might contribute to these pages
accounts of exploration, adventure, and discovery that would
be read with interest. The time will come, sooner or later,
when the dreadful sand of the desert will yield up its long-
buried secrets, and then there will indeed be unlooked for
mortifications for our modern vanity.*

*"The people of Pashai," says Marco Polo, the daring
traveller of the thirteenth century, "are great adepts in sorceries and the diabolic arts." And his learned editor adds:
"This Pashai, or Udyana, was the native country of Padma
Sambhava, one of the chief apostles of lamaism, i.e., of
Tibetan Buddhism, and a great master of enchantments. The
doctrines of Sakya, as they prevailed in Udyana in old times,
were probably strongly tinged with Sivaïtic magic, and the
Thibetans still regard the locality as the classic ground of sorcery and witchcraft."*

*The "old times" are just like the "modern times"; noth-
ing is changed as to magical practices except that they have
become still more esoteric and arcane, and that the caution of
the adepts increases in proportion to the traveller's curiosity.
Hiouen-Thsang says of the inhabitants: "The men . . . are
fond of study, but pursue it with no ardour.* The science of

magical formulæ has become a regular professional business with them." *We will not contradict the venerable Chinese pilgrim on this point, and are willing to admit that in the seventh century* some *people made "a professional business" of magic; so, also, do some people now, but certainly* not the true adepts. *It is not Hiouen-Thsang, the pious, courageous man, who risked his life a hundred times to have the bliss of perceiving Buddha's shadow in the cave of Peshawer, who would have accused the good lamas and monkish thaumaturgists of "making a professional business" of showing it to travellers. The injunction of Gautama, contained in his answer to King Prasenagit, his protector, who called on him to perform miracles, must have been ever present to the mind of Hiouen-Thsang. "Great king," said Gautama, "I do not teach the law to my pupils, telling them 'go, ye saints, and before the eyes of the Brahmans and householders perform, by means of your supernatural power, miracles greater than any man can perform.' I tell them, when I teach them the law, 'Live ye saints,* hiding your good works, and showing your sins.' "

Struck with the accounts of magical exhibitions witnessed and recorded by travellers of every age who had visited Tartary and Thibet, Colonel Yule comes to the conclusion that the natives must have had "at their command the whole encyclopaedia of modern 'Spiritualists.' Duhalde mentions among their sorceries the art of producing by their invocations the figures of Laotseu[1] and their divinities in the air, and of making a pencil write answers to questions without anybody touching it."

The former invocations pertain to the religious mysteries of their sanctuaries; if done otherwise, or for the sake of gain, *they are considered sorcery, necromancy, and strictly forbidden. The latter art, that of making a pencil write* without

---

1. Lao-tse, the Chinese philosopher.

178

contact, *was known and practiced in China and other countries before the Christian era. It is the A B C of magic in those countries.*

When Hiouen-Thsang desired to adore the shadow of Buddha, it was not to "professional magicians" that he resorted, but to the power of his own soul-invocation; the power of prayer, faith, and contemplation. All was dark and dreary near the cavern in which the miracle was alleged to take place sometimes. Hiouen-Thsang entered and began his devotions. He made 100 salutations, but neither saw nor heard anything. Then, thinking himself too sinful, he cried bitterly and despaired. But as he was about to give up all hope, he perceived on the eastern wall a feeble light, but it disappeared. He renewed his prayers, full of hope this time, and again he saw the light, which flashed and disappeared again. After this he made a solemn vow: he would not leave the cave till he had the rapture to see at last the shadow of the "Venerable of the Age." He had to wait longer after this, for only after 200 prayers was the dark cave suddenly "bathed in light, and the shadow of Buddha, of a brilliant white color, rose majestically on the wall, as when the clouds suddenly open, and, all at once, display the marvellous image of the "Mountain of Light." A dazzling splendor lighted up the features of the divine countenance. Hiouen-Thsang was lost in contemplation and wonder, and would not turn his eyes away from the sublime and incomparable object." Hiouen-Thsang adds in his own diary, See-yu-kee, *that it is only when man prays with sincere faith, and if he has received from above a hidden impression, that he sees the shadow clearly, but he cannot enjoy the sight for any length of time. . . .*

. . . From one end to the other the country is full of mystics, religious philosophers, Buddhist saints, and magicians.

Belief in a spiritual world, full of invisible beings who, on certain occasions, appear to mortals objectively, is universal. "According to the belief of the nations of Central Asia,'"remarks I. J. Schmidt, "the earth and its interior, as well as the encompassing atmosphere, are filled with spiritual beings, which exercise an influence, partly beneficent, partly malignant, on the whole of organic and inorganic nature. . . . Especially are deserts and other wild and uninhabited tracts, or regions in which the influences of nature are displayed on a gigantic and terrible scale, regarded as the chief abode or rendezvous of evil spirits. And hence the steppes of Turan, and in particular the great sandy Desert of Gobi, have been looked on as the dwelling-place of malignant beings, from days of hoary antiquity."

The treasures exhumed by Dr. Schliemann at Mycenæ, have awakened popular cupidity, and the eyes of adventurous speculators are being turned toward the localities where the wealth of ancient peoples is supposed to be buried, in crypt or cave, or beneath sand or alluvial deposit. Around no other locality, not even Peru, hang so many traditions as around the Gobi Desert. In independent Tartary this howling waste of shifting sand was once, if report speaks correctly, the seat of one of the richest empires the world every saw. Beneath the surface is said to lie such wealth in gold, jewels, statuary, arms, utensils, and all that indicates civilization, luxury, and fine arts, as no existing capital of Christiandom can show today. The Gobi sand moves regularly from east to west before terrific gales that blow continually. Occasionally some of the hidden treasures are uncovered, but not a native dare touch them, for the whole district is under the ban of a mighty spell. Death would be the penalty. Bahti-hideous, but faithful gnomes—guard the hidden treasures of this prehistoric peo-

ple, awaiting the day when the revolution of cyclic periods shall again cause their story to be known for the instruction of mankind.

Isis Unveiled, H.P. Blavatsky, pp. 599-601, 603, 598.

The above is purposely quoted from *Isis Unveiled* to refresh the reader's memory. One of the cyclic periods has just been passed, and we may not have to wait to the end of Maha Kalpa to have revealed something of the history of the mysterious desert, in spite of the Bahti, and even the Rak-shasas of India, not less "hideous." No tales or fictions were given in our earlier volumes, their chaotic state notwithstanding, to which chaos the writer, entirely free from vanity, confesses publicly and with many apologies.

It is now admitted on all hands that from time immemorial the distant East was the land of knowledge. Yet there is none to whom the origin of all her Arts and Sciences has been so much denied as to the land of the primitive Aryas. From Architecture down to the Zodiac, every Science worthy of the name was imported by the Greeks, the mysterious Yavanas— agreeably with the decision of the Orientalists! Therefore, it is but logical that even the knowledge of Occult Science should be refused to India, since of its general practice in that country less is known than in the case of any other ancient people. It is so, simply because:

With the Hindus it was and is more esoteric, if possible, than it was even among the Egyptian priests. So sacred was it deemed that its existence was only half admitted, and it was only practised in public emergencies. It was more than a religious matter for it was considered divine. *The Egyptian hierophants, notwithstanding the practice of a stern and pure morality, could not be compared for one moment with the ascetical Gymnosophists, either in holiness of life or miraculous powers developed in them by the supernatural abjuration of everything earthly. By those who knew them well they were held in still greater reverence than the magician of Chaldæa. Denying themselves the simplest comforts of life, they dwelt in woods, and led the life of the most secluded hermits, while their Egyptian brothers at least congregated together. Notwithstanding the slur thrown by history on all who practiced magic and divination, it has proclaimed them as possessing the greatest secrets in medical knowledge and unsurpassed skill in its practice. Numerous are the volumes preserved in Hindu convents, in which are recorded the proofs of their learning. To attempt to say whether these Gymnosophists were the real founders of magic in India, or whether they only practiced what had passed to them as an inheritance from the earliest Rishis[2]—the seven primeval sages—would be regarded as mere speculation by exact scholars.*

Isis Unveiled, H.P. Blavatsky, Vol. 1, pp. 89-90.

---

2. The Rishis, the first group of seven in number, lived in the days preceding the Vedic period. They are now known as Sages and held in reverence like demigods. But they may now be shown as something more than merely mortal Philosophers. There are other groups of ten, twelve and even twenty-one in number. Haug shows that they occupy in the Brâhmanical religion a position answering to that of the twelve sons of Jacob in the Jewish *Bible*. The Brâhmans claim to descend directly from the Rishis.

INDEX

183

BIBLIOGRAPHY

Agni Yoga Society. New York: Agni Yoga Society.
Hierarchy, 1977.
Supermundane I, 1994.

Lamsa, George M., trans. Nashville, TN: Holman Bible
Publishers.
New Testament, 1968.

Saraydarian, Torkom. Sedona, AZ: Aquarian Educational
Group.
Challenge for Discipleship, 1995.
Cosmos in Man, 1973.
The Psyche and Psychism, 1981.
Symphony of the Zodiac, 1980.

Saraydarian, Torkom. Sedona, AZ: New Vision Publishing.
Battling Dark Forces: A Guide to Psychic Self-Defense,
    1997.

Saraydarian, Torkom. Cave Creek, AZ: T.S.G. Publishing
Foundation.
The Ageless Wisdom, 1990.
Breakthrough to Higher Psychism, 1990.
Buddha Sutra—A Dialogue with the Glorious One, 1994.
The Creative Fire, 1996.
The Mystery of Self-Image, 1993.

OTHER BOOKS BY THE AUTHOR

The Ageless Wisdom
Battling Dark Forces: A Guide to Psychic Self-Defense
The Bhagavad Gita
Breakthrough to Higher Psychism
Buddha Sutra — A Dialogue with the Glorious One
Challenge for Discipleship
Christ, The Avatar of Sacrificial Love
A Commentary on Psychic Energy
Cosmic Shocks
Cosmos in Man
Creative Fire
Dialogue with Christ
Dynamics of Success
Earthquakes and Disasters — What the Ageless Wisdom Tells Us
Flame of Beauty, Culture, Love, Joy
The Flame of the Heart
From My Heart (poetry)
Hiawatha and the Great Peace
The Hidden Glory of the Inner Man
Hierarchy and the Plan
I Was
Irritation — The Destructive Fire
Joy and Healing
Leadership Vols. I - IV
Legend of Shamballa
The Mystery of Self-Image
The Mysteries of Willpower
New Dimensions in Healing
Olympus World Report. . . The Year 3000
One Hundred Names of God
Other Worlds
The Psyche and Psychism
The Psychology of Cooperation and Group Consciousness
The Purpose of Life
The Science of Becoming Oneself
The Science of Meditation
The Sense of Responsibility in Society
Sex, Family, and the Woman in Society

The Solar Angel
Spiritual Regeneration
Spring of Prosperity
The Subconscious Mind and the Chalice
Symphony of the Zodiac
Thought and the Glory of Thinking
Talks on Agni
Triangles of Fire
Unusual Court
Woman — Torch of the Future
The Year 2000 and After

Booklets

The Art of Visualization
The Chalice in Agni Yoga Literature
Cornerstones of Health
A Daily Discipline of Worship
Daily Spiritual Striving
Discipleship in Action
Duties of Grandparents
Earrings for Business People
Fiery Carriage and Drugs
Five Great Mantrams of the New Age
How to Find Your Level of Meditation
Inner Blooming
Mental Exercises
Nachiketas
New Beginnings
Practical Spirituality
The Psychology of Cooperation
Questioning Traveler and Karma
Saint Sergius
Synthesis
The Unusual Court

Lecture Tapes and Videos

The author lectured extensively over the years on a wide variety of
topics. Call or write the publisher for a detailed listing of available
tapes and videos.

TORKOM SARAYDARIAN
(1917 - 1997)

Torkom Saraydarian was a prolific author and tireless teacher. In his lifetime, he published over sixty books, gave thousands of lectures, and traveled the world presenting the practical application of the Ageless Wisdom. Since boyhood he learned firsthand from Teachers about the everlasting value of principles such as Beauty, Goodness, Righteousness, Joy, Freedom, striving toward perfection, and sacrificial service and selflessly presented this vision to the world.

The author's books have been used all over the world as sources of guidance and spiritual inspiration. Many of his books have been translated into other languages, including Armenian, German, Dutch, Danish, Yugoslavian, Spanish, Italian, Greek, Portuguese, and Swedish.

In addition to being a prolific writer, he was a composer and an accomplished musician having published numerous recordings, as well as a magnificent CD called, "A Touch of Heart." He plays all the instrumentals for his pieces including piano, violin, guitar, and cello, just to name a few of the instruments he mastered.

In addition, Torkom Saraydarian was the founder of the Aquarian Educational Group, established in 1961, which was renamed the Saraydarian Institute in honor of his unending service. Centers are located in Agoura, California and Sedona, Arizona. The organization is an educational and religious tax-exempt association dedicated to right human relations, goodwill, the enlightenment of the mind, and the development of the heart.

Although this book was published posthumously, his vision will live for many, many years through the lives he touched.

SUGGESTED READING

On Hierarchy. . .

The Externalisation of the Hierarchy, A.A. Bailey
Hierarchy and the Plan, Torkom Saraydarian
Hierarchy, Agni Yoga Society
Supermundane I & II, Agni Yoga Society
Initiation, Human and Solar, A.A. Bailey

On Meditation. . .

Hidden Glory of the Inner Man, Torkom Saraydarian
The Science of Meditation, Torkom Saraydarian

On Masters. . .

The Externalisation of the Hierarchy, A. A. Bailey
Hierarchy, Agni Yoga Society
Isis Unveiled, H. P. Blavatsky
The Secret Doctrine, H. P. Blavatsky
Supermundane I & II, Agni Yoga Society
The Teachings of the Temple, Master Hilarion

ORDER FORM

✂

❏**Please send the following books:**

*I understand that I may return any book(s) for a full refund.
We guarantee your satisfaction.*

QTY	TITLE

❏**Please send me a FREE list of lecture topics available on
tape and video.**

Name: _____

Address: _____

City: _____ **State:** _____ **Zip:** _____

Telephone: __(___)_____

Sales tax: Please add 8.5% tax for books shipped to Arizona addresses.

Shipping: $4.00 for the first book and $1.00 for each additional book.

Payment: ❏ **Check**   ❏ **Credit Card:**

_____Visa   _____MasterCard

Card number: _____

Name on card: _____ exp. date: _____

✳ **Fax orders: (520) 282-0054**

℃ **Phone orders: 1-888-282-7400** *We accept VISA and MasterCard.*

✳ **On-line orders: nvp@sedona.net**

✉ **Postal orders: New Vision Publishing**
              252 Roadrunner Drive, Suite 5 • Sedona, AZ 86336 USA
              Tel: (520) 282-7400

Call Toll-Free and Order Now: **1-888-282-7400**